I, Francis

The Spirit of
St Francis of Assisi

Carlo Carretto

COLLINS
St James's Place, London
1982

William Collins Sons & Co Ltd
London · Glasgow · Sydney · Auckland
Toronto · Johannesburg

British Library Cataloguing in Publication Data

Carretto, Carlo
 I Francis.
 1. Francis, *of Assisi, Saint*
 I. Title   II. Io Francesco. *English*
 271'.3'024   BX4700.F6

First published as *Io, Francesco* by Cittadella Editrice, Assisi, italy
in 1980
© Carlo Carretto, 1980

Published in English by William Collins Sons & Co Ltd, London
and by Orbis Books, Maryknoll, N.Y., U.S.A. in 1982

© in the English translation William Collins Sons & Co Ltd,
London, 1982

ISBN 0 00 215352 1
Photoset in Garamond
Typeset by Yale Press Ltd and
printed in Great Britain by
William Collins Sons & Co Ltd Glasgow

I, FRANCIS

Carlo Carretto is one of the Little Brothers of Jesus, an Order inspired by Charles de Foucauld. He now stays permanently at the Order's house in the Umbrian Hills in Italy, where he lives the life of a hermit.

Among his books are *The God Who Comes, Letters From The Desert, In Search of Beyond, Love is for Living* and *The Desert in the City.*

Available by the same author

THE DESERT IN THE CITY
(Collins and Fount Paperbacks)

Contents

INTRODUCTION

Sainthood - Just A Dream?

At least once in our lives we have dreamed of becoming saints, of being saints.

Stumbling under the weight of the contradictions of our life, for a fleeting moment we glimpsed the possibility of building within ourselves a place of simplicity and light.

Horrified at our selfishness, we burst asunder the chains of the senses, at least in our desire, and glimpsed the possibility of true freedom and authentic love.

Bored by a middle-class, conformist life, we suddenly saw ourselves out on the streets of the world – bearers of a message of light and love, love of all sisters and brothers, and ready to offer, on the altar of unconditional love, the witness of a life in which the primacy of poverty and love would make communicating and relating an easy matter.

This is when Francis entered our life in some way.

It would not be easy to find a Christian – Catholic, Protestant or Orthodox – who has never identified the notion of human holiness with the figure of Francis of Assisi, and who has not in some measure desired to imitate him.

As Jesus is the basis and ground of everything, as Mary is the Mother *par excellence,* as Paul is the Apostle of the Gentiles – so Francis, in all Churches, is the incarnation, the ideal figure, of the human being who sets out on the adventure of sainthood and expresses it in a way that is truly universal. Anyone who has ever considered holiness possible in a human being, has seen it in the poverty and tenderness of Francis, has joined himself or herself to the prayer of the Canticle of Creatures – has dreamed of going beyond the limits imposed on us by unbelief, the limits of fear, beyond which one should indeed be able to tame wolves and speak to the fishes and the swallows.

I think Francis of Assisi is in the depths of every human being, for all are touched by grace – just as the call to holiness is in the depths of every human being.

And yet at any moment in history, Francis, while profoundly incarnate in history, can be placed outside history as well.

He can be placed with the first Christians, who, as itinerants in the streets of the Roman Empire, bore with them the joy of a message that was really new. He can be placed among the medieval reformers, as the rebuilder of a Church enfeebled by political struggle and threatened by false compromise. He can be placed in the baroque era, challenging, with his strange poverty and humility, the pride of the clerical class, whose priesthood was that of lords of the people instead of as their servants. He can be placed in the world of today as the prototype of the modern man or woman, sallying forth from his or her anguish and isolation to renew the discourse with nature, with human beings and with God.

Especially with God.

Let me explain what I mean.

If it is true, and it is, that we are living in the most atheistic epoch of all times, it is just as true that it takes practically nothing to reverse the situation.

In the saturated sea of tensions that surrounds us, a sea prepared and purified by our suffering and earnest searching, it takes only a minimal catalytic factor to provoke a sudden and total precipitation. I have become accustomed to seeing more conversions among the 'far' than among the 'near'; and when I am invited to talk of God, those most interested are the ones who have always denied him.

So often a 'no to everything', thickened to curdling by the spirit of free and genuine thinking and searching, explodes in a 'yes to everything' in the presence of the sudden radiation of the Absolute.

Even matter, heretofore seen as empty of God, which would be useless in any event, suddenly lights up with this Presence that was always present and now returns to speak to us of its deepest mysteries.

Contemporary atheism, in its immense efforts to liberate itself from a bygone religious culture, is on the eve of a radical explosion of faith. Naked, and more transparent, this faith will have acquired a more vital capability of contemplating the oneness of the All as a sign of God's immanence in things, together with the perfect transcendence of his triple divine person.

*

But how shall we begin?

How can we find within us the power of believing in the possibility of renewing the world, of finding peace once more and our lost joy – of feeling hope again, of building upon a rock?

We all have a feeling of having arrived at a critical juncture in history, after a long period of a thousand disasters that has come at least to its final agony.

There are those who speak of an imminent apocalypse, of an atomic terror. But even if we do not wish to go that far, relying on our basic hope – nevertheless it is a sorrowful hope, that peace may win out over fear, that fear itself may deter human beings from pushing the nuclear button. We feel ill at ease, lined up as we are behind row upon row of machines, and dismayed to discover that technology has led us into a dark, unpleasant tunnel where we can scarcely breathe.

And what are we to say when one grey autumn morning we perceive, coming out of the mist, the little stream where we used gaily to splash and play as children, converted now into a filthy current of water covered with foam and invaded by mountains of garbage – antithetical symbol of prosperous civilization?

The malaise of which we are conscious at that moment is deep, deeper than we first suspect, and it does us more harm than we think.

In the long term it destroys joy, it takes away our peace. It makes us nervous, and it makes us wicked.

We end up by hating everyone and everything.

And we do not like to think about it, so we toss down some alcohol, or light up a cigarette.

But underneath, it still hurts. And it blocks off the horizons of life.

If we happen to be passing by the school we attended long ago, or the place where we used to work, or even the house we lived in in years gone by, perhaps built by our own hands, with our own sweat and effort – and it has gone to rack and ruin, so much so that we would hate even to have to go into it again – then even daily toil takes on the hue of something we do in vain.

The very steeples of our churches no longer have the power to speak to us, or inspire us.

The only thing that holds any power of attraction for us now is flight, or the desire to taste some new pleasure, even a dangerous one – and we become available for every sort of forbidden adventure.

Even the good fall short. Mothers spend their days away from their children, fathers are continually having something to do far from home. We have started down the slippery slope, and the boredom we can no longer escape results in dejection, mistrust of society or of our own work, dryness of heart, and the cloying of physical pleasures as a surrogate for values now compromised or destroyed.

A glance at a list of the films 'now showing', a walk by night through a railway terminus where the waiting room has become a public dormitory for uprooted men and women, a few hours spent in an inner-city dispensary where addicts gather in droves for their methadone, are all we need to convince ourselves that we have come to an historical juncture of exceptional critical gravity, and this to an extent never experienced before.

Like an epidemic that has reached the term of its incubation, evil has invaded the whole body of humankind. It is above, it is below, it is within and without, it is everywhere.

A few days ago I revisited the Berlin Wall – that absurdity that lasts and lasts while life goes on around it as if nothing were the matter.

I realized as never before that that wall is but one outward sign of an infinite number of other walls, the walls that divide up people and things. The real wall is within us, and it divides rich from poor, nation from nation, children from parent, human beings from one another, human beings from God.

We are divided, split apart to the depths of our innards, as the Berlin Wall divides Germans from Germans, as Jerusalem is split between Jews and Arabs, as any man or woman may be all alone in the universe around.

Everything is quiet, for the moment – but all ready to explode.

Yes, I truly believe we could be on the eve of the apocalyspe – unless...

*

Here I am up in the Cave of Narni to spend a few months in solitude. Once more I yield to the lure of the wilderness, ever the sanctuary where I can encounter the Absolute that is God, and the place where truth bursts out in blossom. The Franciscan solitude of this lofty grotto rivals the dunes of Beni-Abbes, or the harsh desert of Assekrem. At bottom they all spring from the same root; for when Père de Foucauld sought the African desert, he was doing what Francis had done when he sought the silence of the Subasio caverns, or the rough country of Sasso Spico at La Verna.

What counts is God, and the silence of an environment where he is near.

I sought out this hermitage because it is one of the special places of the Franciscan world, where the Saint sojourned on repeated occasions, and where all blends together in a perfect oneness. Forests, bare rock, the architecture, poverty, humility, simplicity and beauty all go together to form one of the masterpieces of the Franciscan spirit – an example to the centuries of peace, prayer, silence, ecology, beauty and the human victory over the contradictions of time.

When we behold these hermitages, the abodes of men and women of peace and prayer and joyous acceptance of poverty, we have the answer to the anguished conflicts that torment our civilization.

You see – these rocks say to us – you see, peace is possible. Do not seek for luxury when you build your houses, seek the essentials. Poverty will become beauty then and liberating harmony – as you can see in this hermitage. Do not destroy forests in order to build factories that swell the ranks of the unemployed and create unrest; help human beings to return to the countryside, to learn again to appreciate a truly well-turned object, to feel the joy of silence and of contact with earth and sky. Do not hoard up money – inflation and greedy people lie in ambush for you; instead, leave the door of your heart open for a dialogue with your brother, for service to the very poor.

Do not prostitute your labour by fabricating things that last half a season, consuming what little raw material you have left; but make pails like the one you see here at this well – it has been drawing its water for centuries and is still in use.

The ill you speak of consumerism is a cover. You fill your mouth with words to stifle a bad conscience. Even as you speak, you are consumerism's slaves, without any capacity for innovation and imagination.

And then ...

Unburden yourselves of your fear of your brothers

and sisters! Go out to meet then unarmed and meek. They are human beings too, just like you, and they need love and trust, even as you.

Do not be concerned with 'what you are to eat and with what you are to drink' (Matthew 6:25); be calm, and you shall lack nothing. 'Set your hearts on his kingdom first, and his righteousness' (Matthew 6:33), and everything else will be given to you for good measure. 'Each day has enough trouble of its own' (Matthew 6:34).

Yet, this hermitage speaks. It speaks and says that brotherly and sisterly love is possible.

It speaks and says that God is our Father, that creatures are our brothers and sisters, and that peace is joy.

All you have to do is to will it.

Try it, brothers and sisters, try it, and you will see that it is possible.

The Gospel is true.

Jesus is the Son of God, and saves humankind.

Nonviolence is more constructive than violence.

Chastity is more pleasurable than impurity.

Poverty is more exciting than wealth.

*

Try to think about it, sisters and brothers. What an extraordinary adventure lies here before us.

If we put Francis's project into effect we shall be escaping the atomic apocalypse.

Is it not always this way? God proposes peace.

Why not try it?

CARLO CARRETTO

ONE

I, Francis

I was born is Assisi, in Italy, eight hundred years ago. And eight centuries later I still remember a thing or two.

When I ask myself why I have survived so long in people's hearts, Jesus gives me the answer in the Gospel, in the passage called the Beatitudes. The Beatitudes are about earth, but they are still true in heaven. And the answer is, 'Blessed are the meek, for they shall possess the land.'

Yes, I may as well admit it. I was meek. Or at least I very much wished to be, and not only that, but I tried to do something about it.

If I were still on earth I should still blaze the same trail. People are tired of violence. They may find it difficult to live in peace with one another, but they very much desire to do so. Instinctively they prefer the lamb to the lion.

I am touched at the thought that anyone still remembers me, Francis, son of Peter of Bernardone and of ... Try to think of the name of my mother. Few know it! But they recall my father's name very well. That is always the way of it. You are still anti-feminists! Yet I owe much more to my mother than to my father. She was French, from Provence. She sang very well. And she loved Assisi better than the natives, because she had taste.

Now I shall tell you. Pica. That was her name. She was beautiful and sweet, and she had faith.

My father, on the other hand, did not have much faith. He liked money better, and it multiplied in his hands with ease. He was a cloth merchant.

Money meant little to me because it had not cost me anything. My father had worked hard to amass his, and ran serious risk of assault and robbery every time one of his caravans went on the road, to France and farther. You have to realize that there were robbers in those days too! One had to take great risks to succeed; be on the alert against being over-reached and often ... not enough.

Yes, money meant little to me. Mine was a different set of values – beauty, song, friendship, glory, and glory especially.

Thanks to my father's money and my mother's good taste I passed my childhood like the classic spoiled child, studying little and having a good time.

But how could it have been otherwise?

My father, who was afraid I would die on him, thirsted for sons for the continuity of the family line. Now he had got this rather delicate boy, so he postponed my education until it was too late. And my Provençal mother, gentle as her compatriots, spared me every weariness, exertion or pain.

Imagine the result.

Precisely because they loved me so much my parents connived to make of me, their own child, a 'landslide' – as the Italians say today, meaning a disaster.

I have to say disaster when I think of what they had in mind.

My father wanted me to go into business. But with the lazy life I had been leading I certainly had no wish to wear myself out in the warehouses or on the streets.

My mother. What did my mother want? I do not even know what she wanted. She only wanted me at home with her, to sing with her and be a good little boy.

Not even she knew what a good little boy was.

What I can tell you is that she doted on me, very much, and on this point we always got along well together.

But in a house like ours what could you do but dote? Good taste was in evidence everywhere, money was the main concern, and all hopes were on me. And I did not know how to do anything.

No, that is not true. I did know how to do something. Sing, dress up, organize parties.

I had begun to make friends in Assisi, and my adolescence unfolded in a culture where singing was everybody's ambition and dressing up everybody's favourite pastime. And as I scarcely wanted for brocade, neither did I lack friends. I was king.

Bit by bit I grew up, and family plans expanded with me. Set against my father's old refrain that I should become a merchant with him, appeared an alternative course much in favour with the 'fine families' of those days – the use of arms, a military career.

Oh, I do not mean that the young men of Assisi were keen to get themselves killed in battles. Arms meant glory, an easy life, prestige.

Assisi was a little town at the foot of a hill between

Perugia and Spoleto. It had no need of arms.

But arms were all the rage. People loved shining armour and horses in fancy trappings. No, these young sprigs always came back from battle. The death of an upper- or middle-class citizen, under arms for fashion's sake, was never a very serious possibility.

They came back for May Day, to show off their glittering armour to the ladies, who were even more enthusiastic than their men when it came to this sort of thing.

Those who did not come back from battle were the poor wretches dragged from prison for the occasion and ordered to fight. Those were always the simple, the gullible, with nothing but a short sword, driven on by their own great familiarity with suffering.

By now it was clear that I was not cut out to be a businessman. Even my mother agreed with me, and had warded off my father's last broadsides. Defeated now in the dreams he had for me, he worried about the future of his warehouse, which was doing a brisk business.

Now pieces of armour began to appear here and there in the house, swords, breastplates – things like that.

The project received a timely fillip from the jumbled political situation.

Lothario, one of the Counts of Segni, had ascended the papal throne under the name of Innocent III. Three months later, in the spring of 1198, the Assisans actually assaulted the Fortress of the Rock, symbol of imperial might, and destroyed it.

Now matters grew more serious. Perugia prepared a lesson for the boldness of Assisi.

And indeed the lesson turned out badly for Assisi. We were beaten.

I say 'we'. Yes, I, too, was there, in the battle, encouraged to go by all the people where I lived, who idolized me in my shining breastplate, and by my mother's smile.

My father frowned at me, and merely said, 'Take care. You have no judgement. You are a dreamer.'

I certainly took care.

I crossed swords with no one at Collestrada, where the encounter with the Perugians took place, and I ended up where you always end up if you do not understand much about military manoeuvres – as a prisoner.

I was not very happy about that, even though basically I had done what my father had told me to do. I had taken care.

But my sense of glory had received a slap.

Prisoner. What a humiliation.

During my year in captivity at Perugia, I came to realize that war was not exactly my profession. But I could not decide what to do with my life instead.

What was left for me if I did not wish to go into business, and if arms – the real kind, the kind that draw blood – were not for a dreamer like me?

It was a sad year. Prison was wearisome, although my family managed to get messages and food to me, thanks to friends in Perugia.

I fell ill.

I passed my days and nights in thought. I lived within myself, plunged into the abyss of my poverty-stricken reality, and I drowned in melancholy.

Never had I been so sad. I think my illness was actually due to the sadness.

Later I knew joy, the true joy of being alive. But I must say that for the time being, I experienced the full depression of youth as I clutched my head in desperation, not knowing what decision to make.

It can kill!

I felt I would suffocate!

The explosive charge of life within me was covered with a thick scab of doubt – un-faith, un-hope, and un-love.

I must have made the Perugians sorry for me by my silence and my lifeless look. In any case they were persuaded to allow me to depart for Assisi. Doubtless they said to one another, 'This poor little lad will never be a danger to our city!'

What a fuss my mother made of me, once I got back! I think she was so happy to have me home with her that she was even glad I was sick.

Ah, mothers!

My mother's attentions, along with the sunshine of Assisi, little by little gained the upper hand, and I was on the road to health once more.

Once I had begun to regain my health I noticed I had changed – changed a great deal.

Sorrow had broken the soil, where a bad upbringing, based on permissiveness and weakness, had only hardened the ground.

I realized that my long illness had actually been a grace.

It had acted as a plough, turning over the earth, breaking it up, and letting the season of spring burst forth.

Above all it had done two great things for me. It had deprived me of my security, and it had given me new eyes.

As for my security, it had really taken that away, making me taste the bitter poverty of someone little, weak, insecure and sick, who can find the path of truth and love only in humility. But what was most important to me was the new way in which my eyes saw things.

I had the impression that I had never seen a single thing before, and I understood what the psalm meant, 'They have eyes, but never see' (Psalm 115:5.)

I had not seen!

Yes, now I saw the sun, the moon, the earth, the springs, the flowers. I had not seen them before.

I had overlooked them, taken them for granted as trimmings to the landscape. I had gazed at them as though gazing at strangers.

But now they spoke to me, I felt them near, I loved them, they moved me.

In fact I could not help crying when I saw the sunset, or the meadows covered with poppies and lilies.

Everything seemed new to me, ever new, and as light entered my eyes it turned into joy within my heart.

I think my first real prayers were said at this time, although I had prayed with my mother so often before. In any case, I am sure my need to give thanks dates from then.

Thanks to the sky.

Thanks to the earth.

Thanks to life.

Thanks to God.

God!

Who was God for me?

Oh, it is difficult to answer that.

I, Francis, child of this Umbrian countryside, had inhaled God, with all my tribe, from time immemorial. I had identified him with the tenderness of our olive trees, with the beauty of our stupendous land-scape, with the light that spread everywhere and suffused everything it touched.

How can one be born in a land so lovely and so harmonious, and not be aware of God's presence behind it all?

Impossible! My compatriots believed in God and so did I.

But what was God for us?

What was God for me?

It is hard to say.

And so all I can tell you simply and clearly is that whatever God had been for me, now burst into my life.

The 'someone' that God was, so far away, whom I had known from my Umbrian childhood, became someone very near, started speaking to me through all the wonderful signs he placed in the sky and on the earth that we call creatures.

I began to grasp that he was all around me, and had sent those marvellous messengers, creatures, before his face.

I felt that he wished to speak to me. So I kept repeating, 'What do you want me to do, Lord?'

This phrase came to my lips with ever greater ease, and later in Spoleto, in my last wretched effort to make a soldier of myself, when I was asking help of heaven in making a decision, I used it as my answer to the voice that kept asking me, 'Francis, which do you choose, the servant or the master?' 'The master,' I would reply, and add, 'What do you want me to do, Lord?'

TWO

The Poor it is Who Save

Middle-class rich boy that I was, I would never have imagined that the poor would be my salvation.

Owing to the upbringing I had received at my mother's hands, as well as the attitude of the church I had been attending until then, I had always thought it was we rich and well-to-do who would be the ones to save the poor. The latter depended on us, it seemed, and our generosity was their salvation. Without us they would have been doomed to die.

What blindness was ours and mine!

The truth was just the contrary, and now life was to demonstrate this to me.

It was the poor who would be my salvation, and not I theirs.

It was they who were to put me back on my feet.

After my long illness which, as I have already told you, had given me new eyes, the poor entered my life on a massive scale. They occupied my attention, educated me.

And I saw them everywhere – on the steps of the churches, at the doors of houses, in the streets, in shelters, in haylofts, in town, in the country, every-where.

If you consider that in my day there were no pensions for the elderly, and social welfare was still a dream to come, the consequences are not hard to imagine.

The moment a labourer ceased working, whether from illness or old age, he was on the street.

The number of beggars increased *ad infinitum*, and society was infected by a plague that neither State nor Church had the wherewithal to overcome: the plague of poverty.

The poor depended entirely on public alms, and on the constant activity of good Christians.

Queens and the rich vaunted themselves on their dedication to the alleviation of poverty, and noble families found in the poor a visible opportunity for the expression of their generosity, paternalism, or, in happier instances, authentic charity.

No country dwelling was without a corner of the hayloft reserved for the wandering beggar. No Christian lady neglected to set aside a bit of bread and soup for those who sought alms to survive in the name of Christ.

My mother, too, was generous with the poor, and gave them many things. I had always seen many poor people in my home.

But as I have told you, when I began to live again, and to see everything with new eyes, I saw the poor with new eyes as well.

In fact it was the poor most of all that I saw with new eyes.

I must tell you that it was precisely they who saved me, who drew me out of the cavern of my selfishness.

In seeing them I found the strength to live, for I found in them my tomorrow, my vocation, the joy of doing something worthwhile with my life.

What is more, the poor educated me to the patience I lacked, to the repentance about which I knew nothing.

Not to mention docility, graciousness in accepting from others, hope in tomorrow, and courage to go on!

But most of all they opened my heart to understand ... No, I shall not tell you yet. I shall tell you later – the name of someone they led me to discover. Wait a little.

*

The discovery of the poor led me to become an arrant thief – abetted in this by my impulsiveness and my rather childish radicalism.

Theft became my favourite pastime. I shall not attempt to tell you how many things I stole from my house during that period!

No drawer, no remnant, was safe any longer. I found, I cut, I disappeared.

I returned with more joy in my heart every time – and with less and less fear of a scolding from my parents.

Of course!

My mother let me do as I pleased. My father was somewhat more strict with me. Especially when he began to realize what a bad turn his son Francis had taken (he declared him to be 'lacking in judgement' and yes, a bit disturbed), he began to look well to his warehouse!

The first time I put my father in a rage was when I had decided not to go into business with him as he wanted; now, the second time, and this was a bit more serious, was when I stole from his shop.

We butted heads. I overdid things, I was a wastrel, while he was greedy and hard and, for good measure, was starting to dislike me. This state of affairs disturbed a mother who was so sweet, who gladly closed her eyes to my thievery, and who kept telling my father, 'Be patient, let him alone, he is still not well'.

But I was well. I was well, and how well I was!

Never had I felt as well as I felt now that I had discovered the law of reciprocal containers, and I would have sold all Assisi to help the poor.

The law of reciprocal containers? Ah, you would like to know what that is? Well, the law of reciprocal containers is the first thing you learn when you begin to notice the poverty around you.

Find it where it is and put it where it isn't.

It is an easy rule, and ought to be the rule for politicians at all levels of government, but ...

A child such as I was makes mistakes in the implementation of this law. I stole, very simply, thinking that was how it was done. I saw no reason for carrying the Code of Canon Law around with me. But ...

Things were viewed somewhat differently by grown-ups such as my father.

I confess that it was not my nature to compromise. And my father was too proud to consider the slightest possibility that his son might have gone off his head.

Yes, my manner of action had caused a number of people to think that I had gone off my head.

And this was what really exasperated my father. More than my generosity wounded his avarice, his neighbours' little smiles wounded his pride. Their knowing looks had begun to hint that Francis, son of Peter of Bernardone, had gone insane. They believed it, too. If you seriously set yourself to follow Christ and the Gospel, people (especially churchgoers, who have solved all their problems of conscience by placing themselves midway between heaven and earth, between enjoying what is 'down here' and storing up security 'up there') will tell you you are crazy, the moment you distance yourself from their manner of living.

As if all this were not enough, in the heat of my enthusiasm I had taken to dressing in rags – so that I began to be laughed at behind my back, and I even had stones thrown at me from time to time as though, having abandoned normal attitudes of mind, I had to be rejected by the community of 'serious people'. Yes, if my father came to the point of hauling me before the Bishop it was not because of his money. It was because he was afraid of how he was beginning to look to the people of Assisi, of whom he took such great account.

As we had now gone public with the matter, I told my side of the story too, and the Lord inspired me to make a cruel, but evangelical and clear, gesture.

I stripped naked, and flung my clothes (which were his, of course) into the arms of my father. 'From this moment forth I am no longer Francis, son of Peter of Bernardone, but Francis, child of God!'

Oh boy, were we something!

I realized I had been cruel to my father, but I felt too that the Gospel was not being lived, and that people were making a joke out of something cruelly real – the poor.

Yes, I had been cruel. But I was young, immature, and for me poverty was still at its first stage – what you call 'social justice'.

Basically I was giving the middle class a slap in the face. My rags were meant to say, 'Don't you see, you are the thieves? That you reduce your fellow citizens to poverty? As for you, Peter of Bernardone, you have grown rich only by squeezing the last drop of sweat out of your workers, and you live and thrive on the tears of those who worked for you before and who now, unemployed and enfeebled, lie begging alms on the steps of the churches of Assisi.'

How genuine, how authentic I felt, standing there naked before the Bishop!

I still ask myself today where I got the strength to make a gesture like that, a true sign that I had broken with hypocrisy and with the rhetoric of those who were considered 'good'.

I do not know whether it was for modesty or for love, but the Bishop covered me with his mantle.

For love, I think. In any case he liked me, and tried to understand me.

What I am sure of is that in that moment I felt I represented all the poor in the Church of the Poor, and I had the impression that until then that mantle had been a little cold – perhaps because it was too rich, and weighted down with things that had no use.

THREE

Our God is Poor

Now that I no longer had scales on my eyes but had begun to see creatures in their astounding beauty, and the poor in their liberating suffering, I felt the need for silence and prayer.

The outskirts of Assisi held no dearth of places to pray in solitude, and whether I climbed Subasio, covered with its great woods, or descended towards Twisting Brook in the meadows, it was not hard to be at my ease, all alone to pray and weep.

I had donned the garb of a hermit. It gave me a sense of detachment and full freedom, and I loved to run barefoot in the fields, with a bodily joy which God had begun to sow within me now.

It was the autumn of 1205, and the leaves of the oaks, ashes, poplars, and alders were russet and bright yellow, and spoke to me overwhelmingly of how I had been born in a land of astonishing loveliness, expressly made for worshipping God – whom I now began to call 'my Most High Lord'.

Below, not far from Twisting Brook, there was one place particularly dear to me. There in a lovely glade, surrounded by meadow, was a fascinating little church. It was poor, built of unhewn stone, and utterly quiet. Its name was San Damiano, and it seemed made for me, as my taste ran not just to poor people but to poor churches.

I made my first retreats there, and as I sat or knelt on the floor, praying in that little church, I could see the gaping cracks in the walls and the roof. The church was falling down.

But in the Gothic arch over the altar was a marvellous wooden crucifix, Byzantine in style; and what spoke to me, what pleased me about it, was the great kingliness of Jesus and the look in that pair of extraordinarily humble and tender eyes.

I spent hours in gazing, praying, and weeping.

I wept so much I grew ashamed. I would say to myself, 'Francis, you are a baby.'

But I went on weeping, and the tears did me good.

One day as I gazed at the crucifix I had the clear impression that the lips were moving. At the same moment I heard a voice saying to me: 'Francis, repair my house! You can see, it is all in ruins.'*

I shall not attempt to convey the effect this had on

---

* Oh, I do hope you don't get hung up about the lips I saw moving and the voice my ears heard. Now that I understand such matters a little better I can tell you about them, and it will help you not to become falsely mystical or superstitious but to accept everything in a spirit of faith.

In reality, the lips of a wooden crucifix do not move. If, for instance, my father, Peter of Bernardone, had been standing next to me at that moment, being so rich and having such good sense, he would not have seen a thing: and especially, he would not have heard a thing.

It was I who did the seeing and the hearing, for I saw and heard in faith. No one has ever been able to explain how this phenomenon, on the borderline between the human and divine, actually occurs. What is known is that it takes place entirely in the realm of faith, hope, and love, and that it is utterly personal.

me. It was like a message linking me to the invisible world, and it sealed a long period of wavering, of enthusiasm and of searching.

I felt permeated by an infinite sweetness, and I went up to the crucifix to kiss it.

I was all alone, and I was not afraid to leap up on the altar to embrace Jesus with my very self.

I do not know how long I stayed there, touching, stroking, caressing and contemplating Christ.

Every so often, amid tears and signs I kissed him, now on the hands, now on the wounds in his feet and side, and my hand tenderly stroked him, like someone passionately in love.

I must confess that in that moment I was thunderstruck at the mystery of Christ's incarnation.

Just as it had been the poor who had been my inspiration to 'rise and walk', so now it was the idea of God's incarnation that became the only answer to all the self-questionings hitherto in my life.

Jesus was the epitome of all: in him heaven and earth resolved all their contradictions in one

---

God clothes our faith with vision, with light, with voice, in order to come to the aid of our poverty and to give clarity to our relationship with him. But the relationship itself has its validity in faith.

It was in faith that Abraham saw the angel, that Jacob saw the ladder that reached to heaven. It was in hope that Moses saw the burning bush, and in love that Joseph interpreted the dream that he should take Mary as his spouse.

But as far as externals are concerned, nothing visible happens.

When Bernadette saw the Blessed Virgin in the grotto at Lourdes, there were thousands of people around her who did not see anything at all.

What counts – what gives value to our relationship with the divine – is the instrument by which God speaks to a human being: faith.

stupendous, vital act of divine unity, satisfying every human thirst.

From that instant at San Damiano I felt myself fulfilled in Christ, understood, interpreted – and most of all, happy.

Jesus' cross was humanity's happiness, love's answer to all the questions, the resolution of every conflict, the overcoming of every tension, God's victory over death.

If the Son of God had died on the cross, I was saved.

All sadness would have to be banished.

Every one of us was lord of the world

Every pauper was rich.

Every heart was satisfied.

Every project was possible.

I clambered down from the altar and began to dance, barefoot, on the floor of San Damiano.

I felt like a clown, crazy with joy and life.

I sang, I laughed, I wept, I rolled about on the floor as if the divine eagle had wounded my heart and I could no longer contain the gladness gushing up from love's attack.

I do not know how long I stayed like this, beside myself with joy. I do know that at a certain moment I found myself standing by a crack in the wall, about the size of my hand, and I recalled the words Jesus had said to me: 'Francis, repair my house.'

I am no stonemason, in fact I had never done a hand's turn in my life, but I assure you that at that instant I felt capable of building a church as big as San Rufino's Cathedral.

So what about San Damiano?

I ran out of doors and began to gather stones,

especially squarish ones.

But I had to pause very early in my work, for some devil-possessed wretch came up behind me and shouted, 'Hey, stones cost money! Those are mine. Go and look for your own!'

The reproaches for my old vice of thieving for the Lord did not succeed in dampening the joy that still gushed up within me, numbing my hands, which, being so delicate, now appeared all furrowed from this toil devoid of calm or prudence.

So I decided to go to Assisi and beg for stones.

My reputation for any seriousness, compromised for some time now in any case, took a severe turn for the worse as I took up that collection.

Look at what Peter of Bernardone's boy has got into his head!

He has certainly gone mad.

Yes, my friends of Assisi, I have gone mad.

But if you only knew my madness!

I am mad with love.

I can no longer help it.

I can no longer resist.

If I but look that Jesus in the eye, I am on fire right down to my insides.

Don't you know that my Most High Lord is God's Son?

And don't you know that he became a human being, and as if that wasn't enough, he became poor, poor, poor!

Just see how poor he is. He has nothing left at all.

He, the creator of heaven and earth, has himself come among us.

He did not send someone else, he came himself!

He did nothing to get himself accepted in high

places, nor did he bring anything along to make himself more comfortable.

He did not hide behind the wall of his might and his divinity, he accepted life as the least of us.

He was God and he became the poor among us, the weak, the wounded, the vilified, the imprisoned, the condemned!

Have pity, people of Assisi, give me a few stones – for me to mend God's church!

Then I ran, ran to San Damiano.

I could not keep away from that place, from that crucifix!

I decided to live there, to be there always, and live by alms and work.

I asked the priest who held services in that church never to allow the lamp before the crucifix to go out, and I undertook to keep it supplied with oil myself.

I felt I could have burned my blood, and I would have shed it gladly to see the lamp burning before that crucifix, which had unveiled the mystery of all creation to me and helped me enter the truth of Christ and of things unseen.

FOUR

The Mystery of Poverty

The Crucifix of San Damiano had revealed to me something very important, something I tried not to forget. And thus it became the standard guide of my life.

Poverty did not consist in helping the poor, it consisted in being poor.

Helping the poor was something fundamental since a function and expression of charity. But being poor was something else.

Jesus had been poor.

I, Francis, wished to be poor.

What it meant to be poor I began to see very clearly. All I had to do was look at the poor or look at Jesus.

Being poor meant having nothing, or almost nothing, it meant not possessing wealth, not possessing things, not possessing money, not possessing security, just like the poor, just like Jesus. And even this was not everything. Even this was but the external, visible sign of poverty.

True poverty went to the bottom of things, and touched the spirit. For Jesus had said 'Blessed are the

poor in spirit, theirs is the kingdom of heaven'
(Matthew 5:3).

How these words captivated me! How I sought to
grasp their meaning.

Blessed are the poor in spirit!

This meant that not all the poor were equal. This
meant that there were those who were poor in spirit,
and there were those who were just poor.

And when I thought about the poor I had met in
my life, especially in recent years, I began to see very
clearly that there were poor who were only poor –
very sad, often angry, and certainly not blessed.

And then again, I recalled very well, there were
poor people who were quite otherwise, poor people
who wore their poverty beautifully.

Poor people who had the conviction that they were
being guided by God, supported by his Presence.

Poor people who were able to love, in spite of their
unforeseen vexations – poor people who were patient
in trial, rich in hope, strong in adversity.

Poor people who were blessed because they could
bear witness, every day, that God was present in their
lives, and that he provided for them as he did for the
birds of heaven, which possess no granaries.

Yes, this captivated me.

To bear witness, to testify, to myself and to other
human beings, that God alone sufficed for me, and
that I did not have to be concerned about anything,
anything at all, like 'the flowers of the field; they
never have to spin or weave; yet not even Solomon in
all his regalia was like one of these' (Luke 12:27).

The thought of being fed, clothed and guided by
God himself uplifted me. No power on earth could
have persuaded me to change my mind. Putting a little

money aside – keeping a larder – buying a house: for me this would have meant a lack of trust in my Lord.

Oh, I would not have proposed this manner of life for everyone. For example, it would not have been the thing for my father.

That would have been impossible. Society had other laws. People had different callings.

I was proposing it for myself, as I wished to be a witness to God's love. And I would have proposed it for those who wished to follow me.

Yes, for some time now I had begun to consider, and desire, being followed in this manner of life. I began to dream of having companions, with whom to share my faith and sing praises to my Most High Lord; and he would truly be the Lord of our life.

This is how I regarded the religious – the consecrated person, the person who had abandoned all things simply to follow Jesus, to be a witness to the invisible God out on the streets of the world.

My choice to be poor, then, was not a social or political choice, but a mystical one.

There was no lack of social conflict in my day or of popular protest against injustices. The country folk were in a continual struggle with the landowners, and free towns like Assisi were constantly on guard against the interference of the feudal ones, against being overpowered by the great cities.

It was right to do this, and people did it.

People have been involved in this struggle for freedom since the days of Adam, and the struggle for justice and perfection of truth and love is never over, involving every single human being.

But blessedness was another matter.

When I, Francis, heard the call of the Gospel I did

not set about organizing a political pressure group in Assisi. What I did, I remember very well, I did for love, without expecting anything in return, I did it for the Gospel, without placing myself at odds with the rich, without squabbling with those who preferred to remain rich. And I certainly did it without any class hatred.

I did not challenge the poor people who came with me to fight for their rights, or to win salary increases. I only told them that we would be blessed – if also battered, persecuted, or killed. The Gospel taught me to place the emphasis on the mystery of the human being more than on the duty of man.

I did not understand duty very well. But how well I understood – precisely because I had come from a life of pleasure – that when someone poor, suffering, sick, could smile, that was the perfect sign that God existed, and that he was helping the poor man in his troubles.

The social struggle in my day was very lively and intense, almost, I should say, as much so as in your own times. Everywhere there arose groups of men and women professing poverty and preaching poverty in the Church and the renewal of society. But nothing changed, since there was no change of heart.

When the poor agitate, and their agitating succeeds and they become rich, they grow arrogant like the rest of the rich, and forget their old companions in misery.

This is what happened then, and this is what is happening to you.

Revolutionaries, who battle for the freedom of the working classes for instance ... But having themselves become the State and achieved power and wealth, they then suppress those members of the working class who think differently from themselves and who naturally feel cheated.

And what of the union organizers in the rich countries, who are the most intransigent of all in refusing to allow the working people of poor countries to share the common bread?

No, brothers and sisters, it is not enough to change laws. You have to change hearts. Otherwise, when you have completed the journey of your social labours you will find yourselves back at the beginning – only this time you will be the ones who are the tyrants, the rich, the exploiters of the poor.

You have the ultimate example, and a serious one, in the people who, by their very name, should be setting a supreme example to the gentiles: Israel.

Israel, as the Book of Exodus recounts, was a slave in Egypt. After a hard struggle they won freedom, and reached the Land of Promise.

And then what did they do?

They became arrogant with military success, instead of keeping account of the words of the Lord, 'Remember, Israel, that you were once a prisoner.

'You were once a stranger.

'Treat prisoners with respect.

'Treat strangers with respect.'

And instead?

What an absurd page in their history!

The very people described by Isaiah as the 'little remnant' have with their own hands made remnants of other people, created other poor people, the Palestinian people for example.

The true remnant of Israel today, before God, is no longer Israel, but the Palestinian people.

What a horrible thing in sacred history!

And going on at this very minute!

This is why I took the Gospel path. For me poverty was the sign of liberation, yes, but of true liberation, the liberation of hearts. This was the thrust that shot me out of the middle-class mentality, which is present to every age, and is known as selfishness, arrogance, pride, sensuality, idolatry, slavery.

I knew something about all that.

I knew what it meant to be rich, I knew the danger flowing from a life of easy pleasure, and when I heard the text in Luke, 'Alas for you, who are rich', my flesh crept. I understood. I had run a mortal risk by according value to the idols that filled my home and would have fettered me, had I not escaped.

Not that I did not understand the importance of the various tasks that keep a city running. I understand, but I sought to go beyond.

You can reproach me, go ahead. But I saw, in the Gospel, a road beyond, a path that transcended all cultures, all human constructs, all conventions.

I felt the Gospel to be eternal; I felt politics and culture, including Christian culture, to be within time.

I was made to go beyond time.

In the quest for justice and human equality, the Old Testament would have been enough. It would have sufficed to read Deuteronomy, the Books of Kings, Leviticus.

There, one is taught how to build the State along the lines of good sense, and the old theocratic mentality.

There one learns perhaps to make war, take captives, divide booty, kill, torture perhaps in the name of God, just as was sometimes done in my day, and is sometimes done in yours.

But the Gospel was another matter.

The Gospel is the madness of a God who is always losing, who gets himself crucified to save humanity.

The Gospel is the madness of people who, in the midst of tears, need and persecution, still cry out that they are blessed.

I had grasped all this, and I understood why the wise and the well-balanced would have destroyed me. So I called on madness to save me. And I was happy to have found the true madness, the saving madness of the Gospel.

*

But there was more, and God explained it to me by causing me to meet a leper.

What a horror I had of lepers!

Perhaps it was an attitude I had picked up in church, where lepers were cited as an image of sin. Or perhaps it was on account of their forced isolation. Or perhaps it was because people were afraid of catching leprosy from them. Whatever the reaction, the fact is that I could not bear the sight of a leper, and would not have dared touch one for all the gold in the world.

Whenever I imagined that I might meet one some day, I instantly banished the thought.

But I met one anyway.

And the street was so narrow that I practically had to bump into him – unless I had run away. I certainly felt like doing so, but the memory of the crucifix of San Damiano blocked my escape.

I froze in the middle of the street.

The leper was coming slowly, slowly towards me, dressed in rags.

He held out his bandaged hands to me and fixed me with a look of sweetness and sorrowful humility.

That was when I remembered the crucifix of San Damiano. It seemed to me that the same eyes were looking at me.

Then I do not really know what came over me.

I leapt forward and embraced the leper, and kissed him on the mouth.

He began to weep. And so did I, with him.

I pulled out everything I had in my pockets and gave it to him. But it was nothing compared with what he had given me, with what he had made me see in that moment and in that kiss.

I had touched the wondrous garment of the one whom I was to marry for ever: my Lady Poverty!

I had contemplated in his eyes the mystery of the Incarnation of the Word.

Now I knew my wife, and in her I felt I loved those whom God himself loves: the poor.

My Lady Poverty, whom I had seen in the leper, was the poverty of the entire world, she was one with all that is little, weak, and suffering, she was the tender focal point of God's mercy.

My Lady Poverty!

Her very humble face was the face of all the poor I had ever met, and who had gazed on me with sweetness and infinite discretion.

Her eyes were pearls washed in tears, but filled with a mystery not revealed to many.

Her afflicted limbs had the transparency of light, and were the only limbs truly chaste and worthy to embrace the very Christ.

Her perfume was the perfume of things unseen, inviting you not to the eros of easy things, but to the agape of heroes of the spirit.

Until now I had thought of poverty as the curse of the earth, a fearful mistake in creation, a kind of forgetfulness on the part of God, an inexpressible chaos which swallowed human beings and made them suffer.

Now I saw otherwise!

The curse was not in poverty, it was in wealth. It was in power, which hardened and poisoned hearts.

Poverty was not creation's mistake but its last page, perhaps the most important one that placed men and women before the mystery, and obliged them to search for God and the supreme self-giving.

It was not God's forgetfulness of us, but his true, raw way of digging true love and naked faith out of our depths.

It was not chaos, clutching at men's throats to make them cry out and curse the day they were born, but the motherly womb that would give birth to them for the Kingdom.

From that moment I had no more doubts: Poverty was the dwelling place of the divine, the highest school of true love, the mighty pull of mercy, the encounter with God made easy, the surest way to cross this earth.

I married my Lady Poverty in desire, and from that moment all fear died within me.

Or rather, true freedom began.

*

I would not wish to cause unintentional suffering to anyone, especially the generous-hearted.

If I insist on the blessedness of the poverty proclaimed by the Gospel, it is not in order to enter into any polemic with those who, also in the name of the Gospel, wage a guerrilla war to bring about a change when the poor are beaten, starved, tortured, humiliated.

I admire Torres, I admire Che Guevara. I admire all

Christians who have chosen death with courage, to defend the poor.

They were not the first, nor will they be the last, for, throughout history, wars called 'just' have always appealed to men to satisfy their thirst for justice.

Even Saint Thomas speaks of the possibility of having to wage a 'just war'.

In my time, the Crusade against the Muslims was considered a 'just war', and the Church itself promoted it.

In your times, you consider as just, very just, guerrilla wars waged against totalitarian regimes, against dictatorships which oppress the poor.

Perhaps the Crusaders were right in my time. Just think of the Battle of Lepanto! And perhaps the guerrillas of today are right.

I am not arguing, and above all I am not judging.

I am only saying that there is another method of combating and vanquishing, that of nonviolence. And I am pointing out that in the Gospel it undoubtedly has the primacy. And I, Francis, consider it more effective, even though it may be more difficult.

The struggle against injustice and outrage, especially those committed against the poor and defenceless, is a basic Christian duty, and Christians are not permitted to be silent, to withdraw, to refuse to get involved.

If they understood, really understood, they would volunteer to die for justice.

That is what Jesus did.

But nowhere is it written that, to make your adversary yield, it is necessary or indispensable to employ the sword, the machine gun, or the tank.

The highest claim of the Gospel is that I can cause

my enemy to yield with my unarmed love, with my
bare hand, as Gandhi did, as Martin Luther King did,
as all who believe in nonviolence do, as Bishop
Romero did in your day.

What a sublime example this unarmed man gave!
What wonderful words he spoke against the mighty,
still massacring his people!

Give a nation a handful of men and women like that
– give the Church a band of heroes with strength like
that – and then you will realize that when Jesus
proposed nonviolence he was not doing so to lose
battles. He was doing so to win them, and win them
in the only way worthy of a human being: without
shedding the blood of others, but by shedding one's
own.

This is the principle of martyrdom, which has never
been lacking in the Church and which is the highest
witness a human being can bear upon earth.

Further than that one cannot go.

FIVE

 The Merry Company

I had never entertained the slightest thought of living alone. Any time I heard anyone predict the hermit's life for me, because I fled populated areas after my first conversion, or because I had donned a hermit's dress to gain a sense of freedom, I knew they were mistaken.

I was made for companions, I was made for community.

Every man I passed, I looked at as a potential companion on my journey, especially if he was young, poor, and knew how to pray.

From the very beginning of my conversion to God, I sensed that there would be many to follow me, since the road I had found was beautiful, and so was the joy that the Gospel of Jesus gave me.

Religion in my day was badly lived. Parishes were only half alive, and were for the most part places of cult rather than of life.

Priests in their sermons sought to terrify people with the usual discourses on eternal punishment, while the Gospel was buried in a heavy and inexorably clerical tradition. There was no room for the laity, married people, country folk. Only the religious counted.

Above all, joy was missing. To be a Christian meant to be sad – especially for women, who stifled their femininity in a thousand fears. True, at carnival time all hell broke loose, in reaction. But this exaggeration was precisely a sign of a repressive culture and immature faith.

And yet, people were so rich in goodness, so thirsty for God.

At the drop of a hat, a young person would head straight for the religious life!

I had scarcely embarked on the path of the Gospel, expressing it as a liberation, when companions surged toward me like waves of the sea.

Bernard da Quintavalle, Peter Cattani, Giles, Philip, Masseo, Leo, Rufino, Pacifico, Silvestro!

What memories!

What sweetness in the thought of my companions in faith!

They astounded and delighted me.

It astounded me to see that they had faith in me, poor, ignorant Francis, and they delighted me by their simplicity and enthusiasm.

They seemed to be madmen. Whenever we met, we would run through the meadows like little boys, singing, drunk with the gladness of the Gospel.

We had found happiness in being together, in the power of feeling ourselves to be part of the Church.

You might have said we had just been released from prison, the prison of our past, of our complexes, of our groundless fears. From the start we had agreed to live as Christ's Gospel tells us, without adding anything of our own.

And so when we had a decision to make, we would open the Gospel at random, having said a little prayer, and then we did whatever was written there, without adding anything.

This manner of action gave us a boundless liberty, and nurtured simplicity of heart with solid food.

Another important element taking shape in our community to be was the primacy of faith instead of structures.

We felt ourselves to be a community in search of God, not a seminary for the priesthood.

What made us one was Christ, and imitation of him gave meaning to the manner of life of each one of us.

Between us, we constituted a microcosm of primitive Christianity: there was the farmer and there was the scholar, there was the labourer and there were those who, like Bernard da Quintavalle, had had to give up a fortune to enter our Order.

There were priests, too, like Silvestro and Leo. But this did not make anyone feel any less a member of the community because he was not one.

On the contrary, I must say that the desire of most of us was to remain 'brothers', since the dignity of the priesthood was feared as a danger to humility, to unobtrusiveness, to the desire to count for nothing.

We truly wished to stay members of the poor, of the lowest.

We lived in a couple of shacks we had found down by Twisting Brook, which served as a shelter for donkeys.

But that did not last long.

A farmer soon came with a donkey.

He was not pleased to see us, and made us move out because we had taken the animal's space and might perhaps disturb her.

So we headed for the woods of Saint Mary of the Angels, on the middle of which stood the little church of the Portiuncula, so simple and solitary.*

There it was a simple matter to build a few huts for shelter.

We lived like skylarks.

Our true prayer was joy. Our true rule was the Gospel, and the certainty that God was guiding us.

When I think back on that time I feel uplifted. I should like to have clung to that way of life for ever, for it helped us to break with all our habits, and immersed us in the utopia of the Gospel, which is an explosion of freedom, simplicity of life, love, absence of problems.

Unfortunately things were not always like that. Later on we too knew complications, books, houses … houses … especially the houses, which we never finished building, and which weighed heavily on the Gospel.

I had reason to suffer and be uneasy whenever I saw building in progress.

One one occasion I actually vowed to pull the roof off a little convent that seemed too large to me, too luxurious for us who wanted to be poor.

This was a permanent dilemma for me, a thorn planted in my heart.

You see, it destroyed the limpidity of true poverty. By building, we were unintentionally diverted from our original choice of following Jesus in his poverty. Our visible wealth was like a weed, suffocating the delicate shoot containing the very presence of God.

The same good sense that usually characterized us

---

* This name derives from *portiuncula terreni* (a small plot of land) where Benedictines long before Francis' time had lived. The little chapel is now enclosed in the Basilica.

became a continual danger to our freedom to take the Kingdom by storm.

Pure love was the only thing that could discern what we ought to do, and, be it said, it was the maddest of us who saw most aright.

We were all pulled in two opposite directions – especially I, who bore the common responsibility.

We were drawn to silence, solitude, prolonged prayer.

We loved solitary places, abandoned churches, like San Damiano, San Pietro, Saint Mary of the Angels.

We would never have abandoned our hermitages so full of silence and peace, where being with God became almost palpable.

We prayed a great deal.

But then too we were drawn to the proclamation of the Word to the poor, the missionary endeavour, the Gospel invitation to call human beings to repentance and conversion.

What were we to do?

How were we to choose?

We held a great many discussions.

Then something happened.

I remember it very well, it was 24 February 1208, the Feast of Saint Matthias.

As I was listening to the Gospel at Mass that day I was struck by the words Jesus addressed to the apostles as he sent them into the world.

No longer do I call you servants, but friends. For all that I have heard from the Father I have made known to you. It is not you who have chosen me – no, it is I who have chosen you, and have commissioned you to go and to bear fruit. And

your fruit will remain because whatever you ask
of the Father in my name he will grant you.

From that moment forth, everything was clear. And
lest there should be any confusion, I doffed my
hermit's garb and donned a cassock, tying it with a
cord. And barefoot I went to preach repentance, as
the Gospel had instructed me.

'Go and preach to everyone.'

Spring was coming. We were jumping out of our
skins.

The desire to proclaim the goodness of our Lord
Jesus to mankind, and to share the good news of
salvation with the poor, burned too hot for us to hold
still.

We split up into groups of two, as the Gospel said,
and off we set on the great adventure.

Giles and I, Francis, took Market Street, Bernard
da Quintavalle and Peter Cattani went the opposite
way.

No need to say that we had arranged to meet at the
Portiuncula. We loved one another too much to be
parted from one another for long, or from the place
where we had found such happiness.

*

The journey was extraordinary.

I thought I saw the Church blossoming as I saw the
meadows blossoming around me.

I experienced in flesh and spirit the extraordinary
words of Jesus:

Do not worry about your life and what you are
to eat, nor about your body and how you are to
clothe it. Surely life means more than food, and

the body more than clothing. Look at the birds in the sky. They do not sow or reap, or gather into barns; yet your heavenly Father feeds them.

(Matthew 6:25-26).

And wherever we looked, what Jesus had said was true.

Indeed along all the paths we travelled, things went just as Jesus had said.

Wherever we saw people, we paused, with great love, joy and peace, and asked whether they needed any help. We worked in the fields, gratefully broke bread with the poor, and proclaimed the Kingdom of God, seeking to spread hope and confidence.

People loved us, and we lacked nothing – not a single thing. We had solved the problem that most vexes and preoccupies human beings: the problem of tomorrow.

We had done away with the fear of tomorrow.

'Each day has enough trouble of its own' (Matthew 6:34).

Saving something, putting it aside, piling it up – would have seemed an insult to the God who led us by the hand and had himself promised to solve our problems, to provide for our needs: 'The Father himself feeds you.'

Finding a farmer who would invite us to supper and offer us the hayloft for the night was an enormous joy for us – the kind of joy you feel when you communicate in love with a brother or sister and discover, hour by hour, the help God is giving you.

It was victory over fear – the greatest sin against faith in a God of love.

Our preaching was simple, so simple. It did not take many words to say what we had to say.

'Be converted to the Gospel and repent, for the Kingdom of God is near' (cf. Matthew 3:2).

Once people had heard us they did not want to let us go away.

We traversed the whole of the March of Ancona. Then, as summer approached, we felt the call of the Portiuncula again, of the promise we had made to meet there.

No one failed to appear. Indeed our little group had grown by three, and among the three was Philip Longo.

There were eight of us now, and once again we settled down near the little Church of Saint Mary of the Angels, in our huts, which we had built in the spring and which had stood up to the rains.

And so we finished the summer in the place we loved most, and we could not help noticing how the people of Assisi were no longer afraid of us. They had begun to take us seriously, and were actually helping us.

I was delighted. And I saw my mother again, several times. She approved of what I was doing, and often sent me provisions, which we distributed to the poor. There were very many poor in Assisi.

When autumn came we decided to set out once more, driven by a desire to consolidate the experience we had had of the road; and we headed for the valley of Rieti, stopping on the way at Poggio Bustone.

I remember Poggio well. For two reasons.

At the time I was obsessed with the thought that God was displeased with my wicked past and had not forgiven me for it.

One night, while I was praying and weeping, I felt an infinite sweetness pervade me through and through and with it came the certainty that God had forgiven me and that he loved me.

I was so happy that I roused my companions. I recounted everything to them, and I made a special effort to share the sweetness of that forgiveness with them.

It seemed to me then that I had the gift of prophecy. Yes, I prophesied.

I prophesied that our company would become many; and that we should always have to forgive everyone, seeing that God had forgiven us.

In the enthusiasm that ensued on that day of peace and sweetness, we separated into four groups, and two by two we departed for the four quarters of the world.

Who could stop us?

We all met again, early in the year 1209, in our little branch-and-twig monastery of Saint Mary of the Angels, where we joyfully welcomed four new companions.

Now we were twelve. I had reason to feel nervous. How could I manage to guide so many brothers?

I was happy, but at the same time I was concerned.

We took up residence at the Portiuncula, in that hospitable wood, round that amazing church that you only had to go into, to receive the gift of prayer and tears.

The Portiuncula was owned by the Benedictine monks of Mount Subasio, and in my time it was said to have been built by pilgrims returning from the Holy Land.

It was dedicated to Mary.

There, when I closed my eyes and thought about my future and the future of the order of brothers that was growing up around me, I realized that I had always considered it as the mother church of all the churches we had discovered and lived in to pray to our God.

Yes, if San Damiano was the place where I had grasped the mystery of the love of Jesus crucified, Saint Mary of the Angels it was that inspired my heart with infinite love for the Virgin Mary and boundless confidence in her motherly intercession.

In my littleness, in which I sought to live so as to understand the Kingdom, I had the impression even then that, to be forgiven, it would be enough to enter this place and pray.

Later, the Lord in his infinite goodness confirmed this.

What a pity you have crowned this poverty and littleness with such a big dome!

And one more thing. Why have you destroyed that lovely wood?

We used to love coming there!

Now it is much more difficult to see how things used to be!

SIX

Clare, My Sister

Yes, companions had come, our Order had new members and it seemed there would be many more. But what about women?

Or were ideals for men only?

The clearest thing in the world was that the ideals we had been discovering and living were beyond our strength, coarse and rough men as we were. But women would know how to live them.

Nonviolence, love of the poor, choosing the lowest place – they were experts at that, we knew.

We each had memories of women in our past – of sisters in our family, the playmates of our childhood, youthful love affairs.

How many reveries, in all of us. Especially in myself, who had made my debut precisely as a singer and jester.

And so the image of woman was part and parcel of us, sons of this wondrous Umbrian soil, as sweetness, goodness and delicacy.

Who among us was free of the repressed ideals of knighthood? Which of us had not sung on May Day for those flower-crowned maidens at Assisi?

Such memories I, Francis, had of women, all beautiful and dear. But one stood out in my recollection above all the rest: Clare.

Clare was the daughter of Ortolana, a lady of the noble Offreduzzi family.

She had two sisters, Catherine and Beatrice. They lived in a palace in the Piazza San Rufino, which seemed more like a fortress than a home.

I had not seen her often, but I knew who she was. She would advance and recede on my horizon like a wondrous dream.

I had been struck by her long golden hair and her determined eyes.

I think she knew me, too. In Assisi we all knew one another, more or less, in spite of gratings and fences aplenty, and once I had been converted to the Lord Jesus and began to hold the Gospel in my heart, I learned that she thought about me a great deal and was hoping to meet me, as though she wanted me to help her.

She had always been good. She had not had my restless past. But she understood me, and now she wanted to meet me.

The times were not easy for serenely innocent assignations between a youth and a girl, but this was one assignation no one could have prevented.

It happened this way.

We met near San Damiano, amid the meadows and lilies, and the first thing Clare said astounded me.

'Francis,' she said, 'I see you are looking for God, and I should like you to help me.'

'Clare,' I replied, 'my Most High Lord has summoned me to follow him, and I am full of peace. Let me tell you a secret: I have married my Lady Poverty and mean to be faithful to her for ever.'

'I guessed that already, Francis. No one but Lady Poverty can make you happy, and I am glad it is so.

'I only ask you to help me. There is a great deal of talk in Assisi concerning the kind of life you and your companions lead at Saint Mary of the Angels.

'I, too, should like to live the same life, the same prayer, and especially the same poverty.

'Francis, what ought I to do?

'I should like to make your rule mine.

'I have so many friends who would follow me. They, too, are thirsty for God.

'Wealth means nothing to us any more. Our days are empty of meaning. We suffocate in high-flown talk and boredom.

'The time has come to shout the Gospel by the way we live.

'Francis, think of us. Do not desert us.

'Ask the Lord if he wants us women too to give him an undertaking to give up everything for Gospel poverty and love of Jesus.'

*

Clare had received firm religious conviction from her mother; and from her father, strength of character: it was not easy to deter Clare.

She had always been interested in the poor, she was not frivolous, and she was made for the Absolute, which is God.

Talking with her, I felt profoundly encouraged.

God did the rest, and things were helped along by the relationship between Clare's family, the Offreduzzi, and Brother Rufino, who was with me and helping me.

Accompanied by Bona di Guelfuccio, her best

friend, Clare began frequenting the chapel of the Portiuncula, where we used to meet.

Our conversation was always of our common ideals, as they ripened in her and in me.

I soon learnt what mettle Clare was made of.

I had never seen the like. In fact I came to see that as far as poverty was concerned she was more radical than I was. For the first time since my conversion I felt I had something solid, genuine and reliable to lean on.

The preparation for her consecration was brief.

Clare was absolutely determined to abandon the world and 'practise the Gospel to the letter', as we had put it ever since the same ideal had conquered us.

'Very well, then,' I said to her.

'Poverty for you as well, daughter of knights!'

There was one great problem, however.

This was no question of entering a well-known, respected convent – an 'ancient and approved order'.

Clare would have to go it alone, starting a new form of religious life with advice from a poor fellow like me, Francis, whose only advantage was his great inexperience.

It would not be easy.

Clare had set the evening of Palm Sunday for her great step.

I had told her to dress as for a feast day, and go to receive her palm from the hand of Bishop Guido in the Cathedral during Mass.

Then ...

Then we planned what ought to have got us all arrested. We must have been mad, completely mad.

I still wonder even now how I could have advised Clare to run away from home.

In the house of the Offreduzzi – as I have already told you, it was more of a fortress than a house – there were her brothers, armed to the teeth and far from ready to let the most beautiful of their sisters flee by night to a wood at Saint Mary of the Angels, there to enter a phantom monastery built of twigs and lived in by the comics that we were thought to be.

And yet ...

That night came, the night of Palm Sunday in the year 1211.

Assisi slept under the moon. There in the house of Offreduzzi someone was not sleeping, in fact was very busily engaged behind the only possible exit from the palace: the door of the dead, the little door that every medieval house used to have for taking out the coffins of the departed.

It was Clare, very, very quietly removing the timbers to open a way into the street.

Outside, Pacifica di Guelfuccio, her brave friend, was waiting.

In silence the pair broke for the fields. I, Francis, with my companions, had lighted every lamp we could find at the Portiuncula and were waiting for the runaways.

Fra Rufino and Fra Silvestro had gone to meet them.

Once the runaways came into sight we all went to meet them with lighted torches.

That procession in the night was something truly wondrous. It was a sign of most joyful hope in our poor life.

We did not as yet have a set ritual for the consecration of a virgin to God.

We did have a large pair of shears, however, which

we kept as a sign of our desire to cut off everything to lighten our journey for the Lord's sake.

I can still see Clare's blonde head bending before me in the little church of Saint Mary of the Angels.

And all around, like glowing coals, everyone's shining eyes.

It was not easy to crop off that wonderful hair. It was easier to place a sackcloth robe over Clare's shoulders and give her a belt of cord and pair of wooden clogs.

The ideal of poverty, accepted by woman, increased the strength of man, and made the beauty of the message universal.

*

I still have to tell you about the hullaballoo that morning when they discovered Clare's empty bedroom, about the fierce brothers' wild ride to Bastia, to the Convent of Saint Paul, which we had selected as Clare's temporary refuge, and of their entering the church to take their sister away by force.

We heard about it afterwards. Clinging to the altar despite her brothers' threats, Clare had suddenly torn off her veil, and shown her assailants her shorn head.

The brothers retreated without a word, realizing that there was nothing you could do with a girl like that.

Later, at San Damiano, Saracens, too, would retreat before her when their armed bands were attacking Assisi and its environs.

One night, a mob of irregulars approached the convent. They found themselves facing a woman who, holding aloft the monstrance, stood like a bulwark to defend the sisterhood entrusted to her maternal care.

Had they wished to enter the convent and work their will on the sisters, they would first have had to pass over her body.

This was Clare of Assisi.

※

Strange! I have often wondered how it can be that, notwithstanding figures as remarkable as Clare, as Catherine, as Teresa, you in the Church are still so anti-feminist.

Yes, I have to say it, I, Francis. You are still anti-feminist.

I cannot understand it!

Are you afraid of women because women endanger your virtue? Or do you consider them, without openly saying so, as belonging to an inferior race, unworthy to touch holy things?

Have you ever thought about it?

Now and then you even forbid them to go to the altar and edify the assembly by reading a passage from the Scriptures. Any man, by virtue of manhood, takes precedence.

Doesn't this strike you as taking things rather far?

Or are you still the slaves of ancient cultures, in which women were of no account, subjugated by male arrogance and destined only to live behind a curtain, like the women of the Muslims?

Yes, now it occurs to me. Look at Khomeini. Do you see what he is doing? Understand the danger of religious anti-feminism and see how different the Gospel is!

I can see (and I was aware of it with Clare) that there is a mystery of subordination of woman to man where the priesthood is concerned. I am aware of it in Genesis, when God created woman by drawing her from man.

I am aware of it at the Last Supper, when Jesus instituted the Eucharist in the presence of his mother.

I am aware of it in the mystery of the Church, the bride of Christ and hence dependent on him, the Eternal Priest.

But none of this justifies your attitude to women.

Apparently you lack the gift of prophecy and have no truth to proclaim. Above all, it is obvious, you are still living in the past.

*

The past is past and does not return.

It has taken two thousand years for the Gospel to start penetrating the stiff necks of men self-proclaimedly Christian but still creatures of the circumcision. But now something is breaking through.

The Council marks a turning-point in the transformation of the modern world, sweeping away all the dead wood burdening the Church.

And it could do this because, after so much suffering, the Gospel had penetrated into its very veins.

Read carefully, and you will grasp the difference between the New and the Old.

The violence of Moses in the Old Testament has nothing whatever in common with the nonviolence of Jesus, who instituted the New.

The political concept of the ancient theocratic state, in which we ourselves lived in the Middle Ages, where faith and culture, faith and politics, were one, has been once and for all superseded by the Gospel, maturely understood in those later days.

The legalism of the ancients is being eclipsed by charity, now conquering men's hearts.

The unadmitted race prejudices of caste have been reduced to dust by the sense of equality proclaimed and brought about in building the Kingdom.

There is something new for women too. Mark well!

Open your eyes to the signs of the times and see the risk you run of being overtaken by reality, which has been knocking at the gates for some time now.

Today, women must hear the words of Jesus as men hear them; and if Jesus says, 'Go and make disciples of all nations', it must no longer happen that man hears in one way and woman in another. And if man can assume adult responsibilities, it is absurd for women only to feel capable of working in a shelter or cooking in a seminary, at the service of their so-called betters, the men.

*

What a lot of re-thinking you've got to do!

And how I would like to say to the women of today 'Go!', putting all my strength of soul into the invitation, and all my anxiety over the immense needs of a world athirst for the Gospel.

Transform your home into an ideal convent, as Saint Catherine did. Let prayer reign there, good counsel, and peace. Let your work be illumined by the power of your vocation to love, to comfort, to serve.

Do not copy men. Be creative, be true to yourselves, in your femininity seeking the root that distinguishes you from them. It is unmistakable, for it has been willed and created by God himself. Repeat to yourselves every day: A man is not a woman.

Waste no time in aping men in the hope of somehow or other becoming like them. Try to get as far from this model as you can. It is not for you and anyhow is badly distorted and decadent.

I think there is a model for you women in the

world: Mary of Nazareth.

It is scarcely possible that Jesus would not have thought about this during the thirty years of his earthly existence, or tried to mould a model for women.

Mary was so close to him!

And paid such attention to him!

And she was the Daughter of the Father, the Mother of the Word, the Bride of the Spirit.

We have thought too little about this exceptional woman.

We have not plumbed the depths of her character as 'woman of this earth', as our sister. We have not thought enough about her freedom, her autonomy, her self-fulfilment, day by day in the everyday.

You women are going to have to be the ones to dig out something of the mystery of Mary, in prayer.

There has been too much sentimentality, and too much useless triumphalism! Especially from men. Especially if they are not married.

*

And one more thing.

Do not let yourselves be guided by men any longer just because they are men. If you let them lead you, do so because they are holy saints, and do not disdain the help of people like Clare – who, though a woman, can tell you things of use and power.

*

Now, to give you a chance to relax a little, I should like to tell you a beautiful legend.*

---

* Maria Sticco, *S. Francesco d'Assisi*, pp. 146ff., Edizioni O.R., Milan, 1975. And here I must insert a parenthesis. It was Maria Sticco, gentle Maria Sticco, who, through her book, more than anyone else acquainted me with the heart of Francis.

Francis and Clare were walking together through the countryside, and it was white with snow. They came to a fork in the road near San Damiano. Here the Master spoke up, 'Now we should go our separate ways.'

It was ever he who pronounced the word of renunciation, which is strength.

And so Clare knelt in the snow, with all the alacrity and humility that came to her spontaneously only in the presence of the Master, and awaited his blessing.

Then, as she rose to her feet, her heart atremble like a sparrow's in that white wintry desolation, human desire forced her lips to frame a child-like question:

'Father, when shall we see each other again?'

'When the roses bloom,' Francis replied tersely, for he too was moved. But he had gone only a few steps when the crystal voice of Clare called:

'Father!'

Francis turned; and the clump of bushes at Clare's feet was a garden of flaming roses. And wherever the two saints cast their eyes, roses were opening in the snow as if it had been May.

*

God grant that we may see these same flowers along the pathway of our life. If we do, it will be a sign of the miracle God has accomplished in our hearts, enabling us to live the blessedness of chastity in sweet daily dealings with woman, now, in every way, like Clare, 'our sister'.

SEVEN

This is Happiness

Whenever I climbed Mount Subasio in the sunshine I had the feeling that my whole body was penetrated by light and, with the light, by joy.

At those moments as I walked along the path, I wondered how I could ever have felt downhearted.

Happiness filled me. It had vanquished me.

For me, sunlight was the creature that best betokened God's presence. For in its journey across the universe to touch and penetrate me, it had travelled the same course as God had travelled when he sought me out to speak to me.

It has never been an effort for me to think of creatures, all creatures, as messengers of God, as signs from him.

I never tired of repeating to my companions that creatures were tokens of God.

> All praise be yours, my Lord, with all your
>   creatures, especially Sir Brother Sun
> who brings the day; and light you give us
>   through him.
> How beautiful he is, how radiant in great
>   splendour!
> Of you, Most High, he is the token.

Yes, he is a token.

Creatures are God's 'tokens'.

They contain his presence.

They contain it, they live it, they express it with crystal chastity, without owning it.

These 'things', creatures, have the power gradually to lead us to contemplation which, as it requires our commitment, is known as 'acquired' contemplation, and is the fountain of great joy. I would look at the sun and smile at it.

Then I would say, 'I love you'.

But I know I had not said 'I love you' to the sun itself, but to the one it betokened – God, of whom the sun is a sign.

This conversation with creatures was a strange business and filled my body with such joy that I felt like leaping, shouting, singing.

I felt myself to be steeped in God, as I was steeped in everything I touched and everything I saw.

Everything was one, and to deny God would have been tantamount to denying creatures, denying the light, denying the real.

Thus there was no denying God, not even if all things had been reassumed into the mystery of his Person, forever transcending the universe that contained it.

The 'Mystery' – which had disturbed me for a time – now gradually revealed itself to me, as one of the most interesting and extraordinary elements of creation.

The Mystery was space spread out round me by God out of respect for my littleness and my freedom.

It was the half-light of that sublime alcove where All and Nothing meet to embrace, forever to deepen

their knowledge of each other, and to unveil themselves to each other without violence and without
burning their eyes with too much light.

The wind was the sign of the mobility of things, of
their inexhaustible impulse to enquire, the voice of the
beloved, arriving unexpectedly, experience of him
who had managed to tear me from my solitude, the
ever-possible caress, composition and shock unex-
hausted by continuous growth.

Thus Pentecost had been betokened by the wind
like a hurricane rattling the doors.

I loved to say: All praise be yours, my Lord, for
Brother Wind.

What can I say about fire?

The words that poured from it were never-ending.
There was nothing I could not see in it as I gazed at it
in the darkness of night, dark as faith is dark, in the
moment before radiant dawn.

Life, death, time, space, infinity, earth, sky, love,
health, sorrow, joy, an embrace, everything – everything could be betokened by fire, even the reason for
life: the inexhaustible gift of self, the warmth that
bursts forth from the slow consuming of the giver.

It was sweet to me to pray, with fire:

All praise be yours, my Lord, for Brother Fire,
through whom you brighten the night.
How beautiful he is, how gay, robust and strong!

*

It did not take me long to compose the Canticle of
Creatures at San Damiano.

When it seemed finished, I called my companions
and we sang it together.

I began truly to taste the joy of praying together.

This was the very reason why God had called us together: to pray together.

And now I must tell you something personal.

Scarcely had I begun to pray than my arms would spontaneously rise into the air.

I felt myself to be at the centre of the universe, and all things, flowers, birds, stars, seemed to gather round to praise God with me.

I became creation's voice, the priest of all that was little and insignificant and voiceless.

What a sense of exaltation!

In this task I discovered my secret vocation.

Few words in Scripture had struck me with such force as Peter's in his first Letter: 'You are a priestly people.'

I was soothed.

I had never wanted to be a priest, and my companions knew this very well.

I kept the true reasons to myself, with joy, for these matters are difficult to explain.

But the happier I was not to be a priest, the more I felt that I was a priest.

It was like a late vocation, and I would willingly have shared it with my whole Order.

It seemed to me that priests – the ones ordained by the Bishop - were in the Church precisely for the purpose of saying to all men, absolutely all of them (and even more to all women, absolutely all of them): 'You are all priests, for you belong to a priestly people.'

So I was quite at ease when praying with arms extended, or when I blessed birds or fishes with the sign of the cross.

Yes, I was experiencing in life what you now sing so nicely (and I thank the author):

> How sweet to feel
> in my heart
> now, humbly,
> love born.
> How sweet the understanding
> that I am no longer alone,
> but part
> of an immense life,
> generous and resplendent around me.

And now, brother or sister born nearly eight centuries after me, and one with me in this faith of the same Lord God, let us continue to pray together.

Here is my prayer of those days long ago:

> Most high, all-powerful, good Lord,
>   all praise be yours, all glory, all honour
>   and all blessing.
> To you alone, Most High, do they belong.
>   No mortal lips are worthy
>   to pronounce your name.
> All praise be yours, my Lord, with all your
>   creatures,
>   especially Sir Brother Sun,
>   who brings the day; and light you give us
>   through him.
> How beautiful is he, how radiant in splen-
>   dour!
>   Of you, Most High, he is the token.
> All praise be yours, my Lord,
>   for Sister Moon and the Stars;
>   in the heavens you have made them, bright
>   and precious and fair.

All praise be yours, my Lord, for
Brother Wind and the Air,
and fair and stormy, all the weather's
moods,
by which you cherish all that you have
made.
All praise be yours, my Lord, for Sister
Water.
so useful, lowly, precious and pure.
All praise be yours, my Lord for Brother
Fire,
through whom you brighten the night.
How beautiful is he, how gay, robust and
strong!
All praise be yours, my Lord,
for Sister Earth, our mother,
who feeds us, rules us and produces
various fruits with coloured flowers and
herbs.

Let us pause for now, and finish later - when you have
learned to bear sorrow by loving.

For my story, too, was a long one and before I
could say, 'All praise be yours, my Lord, for Sister
Death', I had to walk a while, and stay long and
patiently at the school of Jesus' cross.

*

Another fountain of joy inside me was the sense of
liberation the Gospel gave me.

The feeling of having been freed from slavery was a
constant cause of gladness.

I, Francis, had been liberated from idols, from fear,
from my complexes.

I felt happy. I made Psalm 114 mine, and I prayed in its words:

> When Israel came out of Egypt,
> the House of Jacob from a foreign nation,
> Judah became his sanctuary,
> Israel his domain.

It was as if I said:

When Francis left his house,
and began to reason, as a free being,
God became his All,
and the things of God became his love.
The sea looked, and drew back in astonishment,
the Jordan turned about and flowed backward,
the mountains leapt like rams,
the hills like lambs of the flock.
What has come over you, sea, that you run away,
and you, Jordan, that you flow backwards?
Why do you mountains leap like rams
and you hills like lambs of the flock?

What a wonderful thing.

Even nature shared our joy.

It was such a fine thing to see someone break out of his slavery that the seas and the mountains took part in the feast and the dancing.

Are you astonished if the wood of Saint Mary of the Angels seemed to catch fire at night when we were praying?

Does it seem strange to you that roses should bloom in winter?

And that wolves grew tame?

And that fish would listen to us?

No, brothers and sisters, rather be surprised if the opposite occurs, be astonished if you see the sky unmoved and indifferent to your joy.

All is one, and everything partakes of the same feast.

You have only to look. ✳

But to see, you have to look hard.

I have already told you that before my conversion I had never looked properly at creatures.

I had overlooked them as though they were something foreign, as though they were trimmings to the landscape.

Now I saw them.

And I looked at them hard.

I realized that they too were looking hard at me.

Perhaps – why not? – they were trying to communicate, as I was.

Perhaps they would understand me.

So I tried talking to them, and I succeeded.

One day I was crossing Lake Rieti, rowing towards the hermitage of Greccio, when a fisherman honoured me with a live water fowl.

I accepted it with pleasure, then opened my hand so that it could fly away.

But the little bird refused to do so, settling down in my hand as if in a nest.

Then as it happened, I began to pray, and took leave of my senses. Coming to myself later as though returning from a long journey, I was surprised to see the bird still there, looking at me with his little head cocked to the left.

I gazed at him lovingly and bade him depart. But he waited for my blessing.

Then he gently flew away.

And what should I tell you about the friendship I once had with a falcon?

with you, back to your freedom in the wood'. I had hardly put him on the ground, when he turned and jumped back into my arms!

He stayed with me so long that in the end I said to the friars, 'Carry him into the wood'. And that was the last I saw of him.

Yes, you can smile!

You are too rationalistic, you modern people, and this is one of the reasons why you are so sad.

For I have experienced that union existing between nature and the ruler, and have grasped that often, even though it is all around us, we fail to perceive it.

We are blind, and most things escape us.

I think children are more aware of such things. We may not take much account of children, but they are the ones who see best.

With good reason Jesus said, 'If you will not be children ... you will not enter.'

I liked children, and I liked grown-ups with child-like hearts even more.

What a marvel!

What a joy, to be with them!

To be with a chap like Brother Juniper.

I remember him well.

One day, Brother Juniper had received a stiff dressing-down from the superior for having given away some silver bells which adorned the altar, without having received permission to do so.

And Brother Juniper thought to himself, 'My, how the Guardian shouted! He must have strained his voice.'

So he went to the kitchen and made some butter porridge.

In the middle of the night, loud knocking at the

guardian's cell, and there was Brother Juniper, candle in one hand and a bowl of hot porridge in the other.

'What is the meaning of this?' demanded the Friar Guardian.

And Brother Juniper: 'Well, Father, today when you shouted at me for my faults, I could hear your voice getting feeble – getting too tired, I suppose – so I thought I'd make you this porridge to relax your chest and throat.'

To a fresh outburst of fury from the superior, who told him to go to the devil for waking him, Brother Juniper replied, 'That's all right, Father – you hold the candle and I'll eat the porridge'.

Yes, what joy those simplest, most limpid-hearted brothers gave me! I could have wished the whole congregation like them, for I understood that to overcome Satan and the world these were the best soldiers.

The ones who were over-intelligent alarmed me.

I felt that the complex reality of the universe was something that ought to be faced with humour.

It was the best way to stand firm in the struggle.

When, for instance, I saw Rufino, one of the best-educated men of Assisi, preaching in nothing but his underwear before the smiles of the pious ladies, I felt then that it was only with people of this mould that the world could be changed.

And when I saw Fra Bernardo da Quintavalle appear before me after the alms collection, empty-handed, half-starved and excusing himself for having eaten some crumbs along the way, as if that had been a fault, I wept for joy, and felt I was truly the brother of all men and women.

That was happiness.

EIGHT

My Church, My Church

But it was not only the little church of Saint Mary of the Angels, with the woods surrounding it, that was our refuge, our peace and our place of prayer.

It was the great Church as well, the one that reached from one end of the earth to the other, the one founded by Jesus himself – who at San Damiano had spoken to me, giving the clear order, 'Repair it'.

At once I had set about attempting to repair the crumbling walls of San Damiano. But I quickly realized that the Lord's words meant something much vaster and referred to the Church of Rome.

Where would we have been without this Church?

Who would have handed down to us, across twenty centuries, the teachings of our dear Lord Jesus?

Who would have encouraged us in the truth, re-assured us in the path we had undertaken?

I, Francis, felt the need to lean on someone, to be reassured by someone.

It frightened me to bear responsibility alone.

So why not go to Rome and see the Pope?

Tell him the whole story – tell him of our desire to live the Gospel, nothing but the Gospel – and beg his blessing.

Confide to him our thirst for poverty, our dream of being with the poor, of putting ourselves in the lowest place, of accepting the legal status of a pauper, of the exploited, of the starving, of the homeless, of the nomad!

Presumption?

Were we asking the impossible?

How few we were! There were but a dozen of us then. And already we felt it necessary to tell the Vicar of Christ about ourselves.

Was this not contrary to the humility we were trying to live?

No, it was not, and we all set out together for Rome.

It was May, 1210.

I, Francis, carried a simple rule with me, drawn directly from the words of the Gospel, which seemed to me exactly to express our common desire to consecrate ourselves to God in poverty and love.

We went singing and praying all the way.

And our joy spread like an epidemic among the people we met.

Food and lodging were no problem, even though the regions we were passing through were poor.

Everyone crowded round in curiosity, and when evening came there were always far more offers of lodging than we could use.

In Rome we went to see our own bishop, Guido. And it was a joy to hear him tell us forthwith not to look elsewhere, but to go on leading our life in his diocese, since he was pleased with us. He even promised to present us to the Pope, for he was a friend of Cardinal John Colonna di San Paolo.

Innocent III, a true prince by blood, was a pessimist when it came to humankind. His life was saddened by warfare waged all around him, especially by the Albigenses, who preached poverty but spoke ill of the Church of Rome.

I had a vague notion that there would be a struggle. I was insistent on rigorous poverty, and the winds of protest and rebellion that agitated the Church were certainly not going to help me.

But what else could I do?

Was I to repudiate my bride, Lady Poverty, for an approval based on common sense?

No, I thought not.

And then I had these eleven scarecrows standing round me. One look from them would have contradicted me.

But we were poor, very poor, and our poverty was like a slap in the face to the men who now surrounded us.

The Pope gazed at me intently, and I gazed lovingly at him.

'My sons, your life seems to us too harsh. We have no doubt that you, who have such fervour, are able to endure it; but we fear for those who will come after you.'

'My Lord Pope, I commit myself entirely to my Lord Jesus Christ. How can he fail in the promises he has made to those who have abandoned all for him?'

And we withdrew.

We spent the time we were waiting in caring for the sick in the Hospital of Saint Anthony. The Pope spent it discussing us with the cardinals.

We knew that many cardinals were against us and ready to give a negative opinion.

We also knew that Cardinal Colonna was defending us, with a thesis very simple and concrete: If we refuse this poor little man's request, based as it is on the Gospel, shall we not displease God? And if we adopt the position that this rule of his is beyond human capacity, will this not be tantamount to admitting that men and women are incapable of following the Gospel on this earth?'

The Pope sent for us, and once more we found ourselves in the great hall in his presence.

Up there was Innocent III, pale, as if he had not slept that night. And before him, I, Francis, surrounded by my dishevelled company.

The Pontiff gazed at me attentively, as though trying to look into my heart, as I stood there before him.

I tried to defend my dreams of living poverty in the Church by means of a parable, which I had first recounted to my companions.

Warming to my theme, I employed all the strength I had in saying that we ought to be poor, and that this was a witness we ought to give to Christian people.

I do not know what happened at that moment.

It was as though the Pope suddenly changed his mind, as though a problem worrying him had suddenly been resolved.

He smiled, beckoned me to approach, and embraced me. I understood that the battle was won, that God had intervened to assure the Pope we were serious, and had no wish to deceive the Church.

Later it was reported that the Pontiff had had a dream.

It was whispered that he had seen the Church of Saint John Lateran about to collapse – and someone dressed like a pauper supporting it with his shoulders.

Was I that poor person?

It took courage to think so.

And then dreams – how can you believe in dreams?

And so whenever that thought returned to my mind I did my best to chase it away, telling my Lord that I was less than nothing, protesting my lack of ability.

And now we were on the homeward road, with Rome henceforth on our shoulders.

*

Our first great elation, at the approval bestowed by the Pope on our rule, soon gave way to a certain vague uneasiness.

As we neared Umbria our songs grew fewer and were replaced by silent prayer that welled up within us, as we were seized by an awareness of the difficulties we were approaching.

One thing was sure, and we could count on it: God was with us and would be helping us, but the real battle lay ahead.

We had seen no poverty in the halls of the Vatican. We had found no signs to indicate there was any there.

This, I felt, would provoke discussion among the little company trotting towards Assisi, all enthusiastic to live the poverty of the Gospel, but at the same time made up of fellows as simple and raw as primitive man.

I could not sleep at night.

In the situation where we now found ourselves was the whole mystery of the holy and sinful Church, at once indefectible by divine promise, yet capable of scandalizing many, as indeed it did, by its wealth and power.

How could I solve this problem?

What was I to say to the brothers?

I was deeply aware of the loyalty owed to the Church, my mother who had given me birth; and at the same time was aware of the contradiction of shameless wealth, of involvement in power politics, which weakened the message and which God had called to the notice of the Pope in his vision of the Lateran about to tumble down, while the poor shoulders of the poor held up the crumbling walls.

We had to hold up the Church. But how?

We had to repair the breaches. Which ones?

Suddenly I glimpsed the danger we could be risking, young and inexperienced as we were, of turning into a band of malcontents, becoming harsh and sour and quick to point the finger at others' faults.

No, that was no way. We should achieve nothing.

There were too many preachers about like that already, especially in the North.

Jesus surely wanted something different from us.

Suddenly there it was. We were to imitate Jesus, to do as he had done. I turned his words over and how sweet they sounded.

'Judge not.'

'Why do you stare at the speck of dust in your brother's eye and fail to see the timber in your own?'

'I have not come to judge but to save.'

It was especially these last words that struck me and went to my heart.

'I have come to save.'

Had I not been saved? And I was happy precisely because I had been saved.

And now who was I, who had been saved, to criticize those who had not had the same grace?

If anything I ought to have compassion.

This thought completely opened my eyes and sett-led my mind about the attitude I ought to have towards the rich, towards those who had not yet entered into the blessedness preached by Jesus.

The sinner, the rich man dressed in brocade, was poor, poorer than those who were visibly poor because they wore rags.

And if I had compassion for the visibly poor and loved them, why should I not have compassion for, why should I not love, these invisible ragtags – the rich, the mighty, those who yet believe in idols and dwell in darkness?

Yes, I sensed this strongly: the unlucky ones are those who have not yet entered into the blessedness of the Gospel, the joy of being set free, and are still glutting themselves with vanity, anxiety, pride, avar-ice, and power.

Of my father and myself, which of us had been the lucky one?

I, singing free as a skylark and feeling God to be so very near, or he, who went on worrying about his money and other silly things?

Of two churchmen, who was the more fortunate: the one who believed in the Gospel of Jesus, or the one who still believed in the violence of the Old Testament, dreaming only of heads to split for the glory of God? Yes, the Gospel had indeed been proclaimed, but the man who did not live it was a good deal more unhappy than the one who had been penetrated by it.

Between Zacchaeus, entering into the mind of Jesus and becoming poor, and the rich man, parting com-pany with Christ out of fear of poverty and remaining in slavery – whom ought I to consider the happier?

Now I had understood, I had found the right approach in speaking to my companions in faith.

'Brothers, we are younger sons, and such we should remain. The place for us is the one Jesus chose: the last.'

But precisely because the last place is the best.

If we take the last place no one will envy us, no one will be scandalized by us, no one will fear us.

We shall be able to see things better from the lowest place; we shall find it easier to understand those who suffer, those for whom we wish to work.

The only thing we have to fear is pride, the wish for advancement, and the wish to judge our brothers, to strike down with our judgements those already sorely wounded by God's absence and the sorrow sin leaves behind.

Our true rule is the Gospel, and we should consider blessed those who have understood, and who live poverty, chastity, meekness, peace and persecution, as their beatitudes.

If anyone deserves compassion it is the rich, the powerful, the well-fed, on whom there weighs the terrible word of God, 'Woe to you!'

*

The Fourth Beatitude in the Gospel of Matthew, 'Blessed are the merciful', was now the light of my path.

Mercy for sinners.

Mercy for Christians.

Mercy for the Church.

Mercy for Popes.

Mercy for our own selves, who had the desire to be

poor but who did not know quite how to succeed.

Yes, even the Church needed to be looked at with mercy. Even the Vatican.

Until now I had not properly understood what the mystery of the Church consisted of: sinfulness and infallibility; bad example and safety on the march along the road; fearful blindness in the shepherds, and the certainty of reaching the Promised Land with them.

Now I saw, and I was glad to have been in Rome and to have had Rome's approval.

I felt at peace.

I felt myself to be on solid rock.

I felt myself to be within God's design.

That God of Abraham, Isaac and Jacob, who had made a pact with humanity.

That God of Moses, who had led his people from slavery to the Promised Land.

That God of David, who despite the monstrous sins of his whole dynasty had said, 'On your throne I shall place a king who will never fail.'

That God of an Israel living with the certainty of the divine promise: 'Fear not, I shall be with you. I shall lead you. You will conquer!'

The infallibility of the Church did not rest on the weakness of human beings, but on the divine omnipotence.

It was not the result of human virtue, but of God's love which, in spite of mankind's little virtue and infantile mistakes, would eventually succeed, by his invincible will, in leading his people to their goal.

In establishing Moses, Saint Peter, and Innocent III as heads of his people, God did not remove the rigidity from their mind or the dross from their heart, but despite the rigidity and dross, he guaranteed to his people that they would reach the Kingdom.

Hence it was not a matter of switching leaders and founding another Church, but of believing that the Church had already been founded, and that we should trust in the Spirit that was guiding it, as he had guided Moses, as he had guided David, as he had guided Peter, and as he now was guiding Innocent III, whom we had seen in all his weakness only a few days before.

Yes, what was needed was to believe that the Church had already been founded before we appeared on the scene, and that we should not have done better than the others.

Perish the thought that we should have been more competent because we were badly dressed and lived in huts!

Perish the temptation to think that, once we had come on the scene, things would have taken a sharp turn for the better!

No.

We, as the Church, would have gone on being saints and sinners, capable of high ideals and base enormities, the dwelling place of peace and a jungle of violence.

All would have depended on personal sanctity, on the commitment and prayer of holy people, on the sacrifice of the humble, on the true love of Christ's followers.

But one thing was sure: even if we had failed, overwhelmed by our sins and our faithlessness, the Church would not have failed, any more than God's people failed in the wilderness or in the terrible loneliness of Babylon.

The 'little remnant' would have arrived none the less.

God himself was the guarantor.

*

My Church, my church,
homely as you are
you are ever my Church!

This is what I would sing, to my guitar, were I to come one night to Assisi to see how things are going.

And I would mean it for the great Church as well as for the little church that is mine, the Franciscan one.

You see, I would invite the sleepy friars who came to meet me, to see their Saint Francis once again, 'Let us go up to the Rock and walk a while'.

The moon is bright tonight. Of course, no one notices the moon any more, now that the local council has arranged for your houses to have this truly amazing lighting system. I must admit your houses are very beautiful, and that the floodlights show them nicely. It is a pleasure to look at them.

While I was alive I would never have thought you could transform Assisi into such a gracious and harmonious little city.

What marvels these basilicas are!

Good job, Friars!

I, Francis, have too much taste not to admire the unity and elegance in the architecture of your convents.

It would be easy to reproach you about certain things which are not exactly to my taste, but I shall not do so.

I, too, have matured over the years, and I would

not now knock convents down as I did in the old days.

Eight centuries have gone by, and poverty can take different forms. I was such a dreamer in those days that I was abruptly replaced by a nondreamer, Fra Elias.

Yes, you can reproach me, I do not mind. Only I ask you not to overdo it. A certain tell-tale who works in a bank, a Franciscan Tertiary, has mentioned to me that your accounts there are rather large.

And I intend to go into the matter, although I shall also have to reprove my Tertiary for violating banker's confidentiality.

But I do ask you one thing.

If you do have money, spend it well. Spend it on the poor, whom we have loved so much, you and I.

If I come to Assisi during the centenary dressed as a pilgrim – and I shall – do not tell me you have no room and shut the door in my face.

Lodge me, as someone poor. Give me work to do, but lodge me.

How horrible that you, of all people, should shut the door in the face of the poor who cannot pay.

Do you not agree?

And something else.

If you lodge me, allow me to pray with you. In the morning and in the evening.

In the morning we can say Lauds together. And I hope we can do this without having to hear, 'This fresco, ladies and gentlemen, dates from the fifteenth century'.

And in the evening, if we assemble with the tourists to pray, and sing Vespers together, I beg you, see that silence is observed.

This is important, and there are people who like it.

You see, if people do not find a mature spiritual atmosphere, after they have left they speak ill of you, and say that you have turned the Church into a museum and give yourselves airs posing as tourist guides.

This is not right. Do you not agree?

But why are you staring at me? Are you upset?

Do you want a sterner sermon?

I gave you one – eight hundred years ago. This time I shall content myself with less.

Besides, I too have learned something, in the course of those centuries, and I should like to pass it on.

On the question of poverty, judgements are hard to make.

The pauper's garb, small house, wooden table, chipped cup, plaited haversack – these are external signs. And then there is the reality, true poverty, which is altogether invisible.

Today, I am keener on the reality and can see it more clearly in depth since it has become more widespread, more universal.

Those who cannot meet the rent are not the only poor. People who suffer from cancer are poor too.

Those who live in derelict slums are not the only poor. Those on drugs, on the fringe of society, alone, are poor too.

And then there is another thing that disgusts me, which we would not have dreamed of doing in my day, but you do it.

You have begun to cheat where poverty is concerned.

In fact, it has become fashionable for young people to dress badly, wearing working clothes even though they like grand surroundings.

And then there are people who actually prefer old cups and old tables as 'antiques', as rarities.

So it is hard to judge.

And I do not want to judge.

So all I say is, place yourselves directly before God and be judged by him.

And keep one thing in mind.

At the vespers of your life you will be judged by your love, not by your poverty.

I say this because out on the frontiers of the Church poverty has become a battlefield, where the poor hate the rich, and the worker the employer.

This is no longer blessedness and certainly not the Gospel. It is Marxism.

Have you still not realized how easy it is to inhale the spirit of the times? And the spirit of the times is not the spirit of the Gospel.

There is no appreciable difference now between a union organizer who is Christian and one who is of another culture altogether.

This is sad, very sad. Is prophecy dead?

Never forget, God is love. Poverty is only his garment.

So do not attack the garment unless you are still capable of seeing, supporting and loving the person who wears it,

> even if he is a sinner,
> even if he is middle-class,
> even if he, dare I say it, is a bishop or monsignor.

*

One more thing comes to mind. Forgive me if I insist on it.

You are living in strange, contradictory, ambiguous times.

You have more wealth than before, and you talk more about poverty. You are middle-class and you play 'poor Church'. You talk more about community, and you live more isolated, more divorced lives.

'Many a slip 'twixt the cup and the lip,' they say – and there is a whole ocean of slips between what you say and what you do.

It is the ocean of your chatter, and you are drowning in it at all levels.

This is why I do not feel like giving you a 'tough talking-to'. Because you are the tough ones, not I.

All one has to do is to listen to you at your meetings.

It is terrible, how hard, unyielding and radical you are.

What a pity that this hardness, this radicalism, is always directed at others and never at yourselves.

You seem to be obsessed by the thought of converting other people!

And I, Francis, tell you: aim at converting yourselves and you will then find you understand things better.

Above all, understand this: it is useless to think you can change the Franciscans, the Capuchins, the Conventuals and ... for good measure, the Jesuits, the Salesians, the Little Brothers ....

It is simply not possible!

What is possible is the conversion of the individual, especially if that individual happens to be you listening to me at this moment.

History has its own laws, and no institution escapes the tooth of time, however holy and great its founder.

Only the naked individual, as naked as may be, can escape the tooth of time, if he can confront the nakedness of the Gospel and make it his.

My children – for so I shall call you, if you call me Father Francis – do not believe in reforming your Order. Believe in reforming yourselves.

My brothers and sisters – for so I shall call you, if you call me Brother Francis – be holy, and the world will seem holy to you.

NINE

The Eloquence of Signs

One thing I grasped very soon after my conversion to the Gospel. It was the power of signs.

I had joyfully realized that everything around me was a sign of God, his token, and I could no longer look at anything without thinking of him, my Most High and good Lord.

Indeed, I felt immersed in him day and night, and no power on earth could distract me from that Presence, so sweet, so strong, so real. It was in this school that I learned to understand and live something very important, a fundamental lesson.

Since he established signs of himself to speak to us, to explain things, so we, too, ought to do the same, whether to avoid wasting time, or to keep check on ourselves along our path and correct our weaknesses.

Yes, establish signs, as reminders of the stages in our thinking, as witnesses to what we hoped to be, as markers to the way we lived the Gospel.

I recall one of the first signs that occurred to my mind. This, I felt, would clearly indicate a scorn of money and victory over greed.

Bernard da Quintavalle and Peter Cattani had come to join me.

Bernard was very wealthy, and Peter was a priest and canon.

'Open the gospel at random,' I said to them, 'and read.'

And what they read was, 'If you wish to be perfect, go, sell what you have, give it to the poor, then come follow me.'

Brothers, have you understood what the Lord wishes?

Yes.

They went. Bernard sold his possessions and Peter renounced his prelacy.

I can still see that May morning in 1208, in Saint Peter's Square in Assisi.

Bernard had a quantity of stuff. I began with the money, distributing that.

What a hullaballoo ensued!

People were appearing from everywhere and nowhere. There were the poor, and the not so poor. Everyone was snatching things up. What a sight!

And we gave it all away, to the very last penny.

What a joyous sense of liberation I felt that morning. And I saw, in that sign, all mankind's enslavement to money.

Another sign which I tried, in my simplicity, to establish for my brothers and myself, was when I had asked Fra Rufino to go and preach in Assisi.

Listen to what happened, in the lovely language of *The Little Flowers of Saint Francis*. Rufino replied:

'Reverend Father, I pray you to excuse me and send me not, because, as you know, I have not the grace of preaching, but am simple and stupid.'

Saint Francis then said:

'Since you have not obeyed promptly, I command you by holy obedience to go to Assisi, naked as you were born, in nothing but your underpants, enter a church, and preach to the people naked.'

At this command, the said Fra Rufino undressed and went to Assisi, and entered a church; and, having made a reverence to the altar, ascended the pulpit and began to preach.

At this the children and men began to laugh, and said, 'Now see, those men do so much penance that they have become fools and lost their wits.'

In the meanwhile Saint Francis, thinking over the prompt obedience of Fra Rufino, who was one of the best-bred men of Assisi, and of the hard command which he had given him, began to reproach himself, saying, 'Whence comes your great presumption, son of Peter of Bernadone, you worthless little man, to order Fra Rufino to go and preach naked to the people as though he were a madman? By God, now prove in yourself what you impose on others.'

And immediately, in fervour of spirit, he too stripped naked and went to Assisi to preach.

I need not relate the rest, for you know what happened. But I am sure Rufino and I were long remembered for those sermons.

At the time, I was much exercised about confidence in God, the simplicity which ought to govern our relations with him, and our certainty about being guided by him and being borne like little children in his arms.

Listen to this sign:

> Saint Francis was walking along a road one day with Fra Masseo. And the said Fra Masseo had gone on a little ahead. Arriving at a crossroads, at which one could go either to Florence or Siena or Arezzo, Fra Masseo said:
>
> 'Father, which way shall we go?'
>
> And Saint Francis replied, 'By whichever way God wishes'.
>
> Said Fra Masseo, 'But how shall we know God's will?'
>
> Saint Francis replied: 'By the sign which I shall show. Hence I command you by this merit of holy obedience, that, at this crossroads, where you are now standing, you turn round and round as children do, and do not stop turning until I say so.'
>
> Then Fra Masseo began turning round, and did it so often that, through giddiness of head, he fell several times to the ground; but as Saint Francis had not told him to stop, and as he wished to be faithfully obedient, he kept on getting up again.
>
> At last, when he was turning at high speed, Saint Francis said, 'Stand still and do not move'.
>
> And he stood still. And Saint Francis asked him, 'Which way are you facing?'
>
> Said Fra Masseo: 'Towards Siena'.
>
> Said Saint Francis: 'This is the way God wishes us to go.'
>
> Having taken that road, Fra Masseo marvelled mightily that Saint Francis had made him behave like a child and he grumbled to himself ...

I, Francis, can assure you that Fra Masseo had ample

opportunity afterwards to understand that God indeed had intervened in the choice we made by such strange means and in such a child-like spirit.

For at Siena, three rival factions were at one another's throats.

On our arrival they were willing to listen to us, and we spoke with simplicity and ardour.

God did the rest, and there was peace that day in Siena.

*

Another sign which it happened I should place before my brothers, so that they would remember to treat everyone gently, even robbers, was at the recently built cloister of Monte Casale, where I had installed as guardian a dear little brother called Agnolo.

There were three robbers roving the countryside, who happened one day on our convent.

Fra Agnolo recognized them, and drove them away with expressions suited to the occasion.

When I, Francis, arrived with the alms I had been collecting, which besides bread included a fine jug of wine, I came to hear about the way in which Fra Agnolo had driven off the robbers.

I reproved him; and to help him remember that God can do all things, and that we are not called to judge, not even robbers, said ...

> 'Seeing, therefore, that you have acted against charity and contrary to the Gospel of Christ, I command you by holy obedience immediately to take this wallet of bread, which I have received, and this flask of wine, and go quickly after them uphill and down dale, until you find them; and present them with this bread and wine from me;

and then, kneeling before them, humbly confess your fault in having been harsh to them; and then beg them from me not to do evil any more but to fear God and not sin against their neighbour; and if they will do this, I promise to provide for their needs.'

While Fra Agnolo went to carry out this command, Saint Francis betook himself to prayer, and entreated God to soften the hearts of those robbers and to convert them to repentance. And so it befell.

*

Placing signs.

Setting up signs that speak to us, that call us back to truth and love.

The entire liturgy is a living sign, a luminous recall to things invisible.

When you light the Paschal candle, the sign of Christ's presence dead and risen, the assembly is drawn gently by that sign to remember Jesus, who is consumed in giving light. In the same way, by giving a sign of our scorn for money, we help our fellow men to understand what it means to be set free from idols.

Just as, at Mass, you prostrate yourselves humbly before the Eucharistic Sign and renew your own and others' faith in the value of littleness before God, so that sign of the naked sermon, humbly accepted, recalled my brothers to the true meaning of obedience.

Setting up signs.

In our days we abruptly set up the sign of alms.

I would have preferred to have set up the sign of work as well for our kind of religious life. But this could not be done. Work, in my day, was a luxury – I mean, paid work, a job, like having a job in a bank is for you today.

If we were to reach the poor we had to accept the life of a beggar, and we accepted it to the hilt.

In setting up this sign we were telling the Church where the problem lay; and to the beggars we were saying, 'Take heart! Here we are, right beside you.'

But today this sign is out of place. No friar with any sense should feel it necessary to go begging for alms while there are no labourers in the fields. To beg our bread as an alms when we can earn it by working makes no sense at all and can become a scandal.

Hence today, a good sign to set up for anyone loving the poor is work, especially a hard, dirty, ill-paid job.

What a pity that some ecclesiastics are so allergic to the notion of manual work for priests.

But they have every excuse.

They come from a school of thought where work was considered incompatible with nobility and holiness. What can you do?

It is a last remnant of the past. The ancient Greeks also scorned manual labour, and the middle class has never been enthusiastic about being dog-tired in dirty clothes.

In my day a prelate would have been ashamed to carry a sack on his back down a street or to work on a building site.

What is astonishing is the ease with which the ecclesiastical world forgets the working-class origin of Christ, to the point of ridiculously asserting that it is 'not right' for priests to do 'manual labour'. This is serious, semi-equivalent to saying, 'It is not right for Jesus to be a carpenter.'

And I, Francis, say this without malice.

*

Another sign, which our convents set up, was the sign of asylum, of protection, of help for anyone in trouble.

Just as a hunted man took refuge in a church, and no one would have dared to strike him down, so the poor felt our houses to be places of refuge, where they could find bread, comfort and friendship.

This was our true glory, and I must confess that the whole Church came to be marked by this recall to charity.

And this is still true today.

Every Christian house, every convent or monastery, every bishop's palace, should keep a door open to welcome those in trouble

And, if possible, the door should be easy to find and not too frightening for the poorest, with halls not too brilliant, staircases not too mammoth – signs rather of might and grandeur than of humility and truth.

*

In my rather childish enthusiasm I often dreamed of selling off the Vatican and giving the proceeds to the poor. I dreamed of telling the Church that it was time to start being serious, to start matching proclamation of the Word with deeds.

Now I, too, am grown up, and just as I no longer feel ill at ease when I see a big religious house, so too I can take a tour of the Vatican without flying into a rage.

But I am still just as convinced as I was eight centuries ago of the effectiveness of the signs which I set up for the guidance of my brothers – and so I feel I ought to tell you one more thing.

And here, too, no polemics.

Imagine a group of pilgrims arriving in Rome, all joyful at the prospect of being able to pray in such beautiful basilicas, and of seeing the Pope and hearing his voice as if he were Jesus.

Well ...

How do you think that – besides the Gate of the Bell,

besides the Gate of Bronze,

besides the Gate of Saint Anne,

besides the entrance to the museum

– they would like to find a little gate, bearing the inscription: 'Come to me, all you who labour and are overburdened, and I will give you rest'? (Matthew 11:28).

And to be able to go in and find a simple place, a poor place, but inviting and comfortable, where they would actually meet a man or woman who would give them the sense of a Church alive and open to the poor?

Oh, it is not that charity is lacking in the Vatican, or in your works either.

I would put it this way. In all the great work of charity, what is often lacking is the sign.

Or if it is not actually lacking, the sign is often too big and showy, too efficient, and the poor are unable to take it in – like an apostolic nunciature, a radio station, a cathedral, and a cardinal's apartment – all at a glance.

Humanity today is sensitive to small signs, concrete clever ones, and especially those that are the fruit of a love that is immediate and lived today, with strength and constancy.

Pope Wojtyla lifting a child in his arms above the heads of the crowd, prostrating himself to kiss the earth, weeping at some scene of suffering, entering an African hut or a South American shanty, sets up signs that speak for themselves and put him in communion with the poor.

Is this not so?

And this is why I tell you that if I come to Rome, hidden in a group of pilgrims, I shall be looking at those famous walls to see whether there is a little door open in them that would fit me, Francis of Assisi.

TEN

The Primacy of Nonviolence

When I, Francis, happen to read the things which you have written about me since my death – so prolifically and in such indisputably good taste – I have to confess that I like the account in the *Little Flowers* best.

I feel comfortable there.

Sometimes it happens that I can no longer recall whether the things related by the author actually were like that, or have been exaggerated – or just made up – but that is unimportant.

I like them.

Even if they did not happen like that, they are beautiful and good told that way. I accept them all, for they give a photograph of me which, even if retouched by your generosity, is a photograph of nonviolence, a picture which I am honoured to accept, and I thank you for having understood me.

Yes, that is what I was, nonviolent. And the *Little Flowers* are a beautiful dream for you and for me.

Deep within us, every one of us, are dreams of such a world, pacified by love and the sweetness of humility.

Is this not so?

Some of you may be inclined to smile at the episode of the wolf of Gubbio. But if you have ever been a child, truly a child, you too must surely have wanted to solve problems the same way as I solved them at Gubbio that frosty morning in the new-fallen snow.

What parables there are for mankind in that wolf fleeing from violence and finding himself in trouble from hunger!

I have to admit, brothers, that I had daydreamed about an incident like that years before, as a boy. I had been told that up there on the crests of the Apennines were ravening wolves that came down to threaten the flocks.

I did not know Christ then.

And yet I dreamed of going to find such a beast, armed only with caresses. And the beast would have stood still.

And now that I knew the caresses of Jesus, how could I have been afraid?

Would I have armed myself with a pruning knife?

Would I have wanted to see blood, even a wolf's blood, on the rocks of Gubbio?

No, brothers, I was not afraid.

Not since I had experienced the fact that my God is the wolf's God too.

What is extraordinary in the incident of the wolf of Gubbio is not that the wolf grew tame, but that the people of Gubbio grew tame, and that they ran to meet the cold and hungry wolf not with pruning knives and hatchets but with bread and hot porridge.

This is the miracle of love: to discover that all creation is one, flung out into space by a God who is a Father, and that if you present yourself as he does, unarmed and peaceably, creation will recognize and meet you with a smile.

This is the principle of nonviolence, and I want to recommend it to you with all the enthusiasm I can command.

I have asked you not to talk too much about poverty today, in view of the ambiguity of your environment and the difficulty in defining your position, surrounded as you are by bourgeois and socialist cultures. Instead, and I say this most emphatically: talk about nonviolence, be apostles of nonviolence, become nonviolent.

Now is the hour, and it may even be the last one, sitting as you are on a stockpile of bombs which you can blow up at any moment.

Do not underestimate the danger. I have a strong feeling that you will have to suffer a thing or two before the end of this century.

You had better be prepared. And better still, hope for the conversion of mankind.

Even Nineveh was converted and saved.

Listen to me.

Today, when you talk nonviolence, everyone understands what you are talking about. The argument is clear and simple and, if put into practice, can change the face of the earth.

You talk a great deal today about human rights, and this is good.

Now, the first human right is not to be subjected to violence, to be left in peace.

The argument is biblical in scope, and you should live it to the hilt.

But it is even broader than that. Much broader, in fact.

First of all, nonviolence concerns the natural world, the skies, the seas, the mines, the forests, air, water, the home.

These are the first not to violate, yet you have sinned on such a colossal scale that I do not know whether or not you can still be saved.

You have violated the forests, defiled the seas, plundered everything like bandits.

Your contempt for nature knows no bounds.

If there were a court of the skies, or the seas, or the mines, you would all (almost all) be sentenced to death.

And perhaps there is such a court. An invisible one. For your punishment has certainly begun.

You can scarcely breathe your air. Your food has become unhealthy. Cancer assaults you with unerring accuracy.

And now that you have destroyed nearly everything, you have appointed me patron saint of ecology. You must admit it is a little late.

I do not know what I can do about it.

What is wrong is that the same people always do the governing: the powerful, the rich, the professional politicians.

Try putting little people in government - the simple, the poets!

But who believes in poets?

Try being governed by those who can still look at the stars at night, or spend an hour watching a beetle under a dry leaf in the forest, or dream over a glow-worm in a wheat-field in May.

They would see humanity's problems better. At least they would not commit such horrors.

You have reached the point of no return. And you have no reason to complain: the irresponsibility was yours.

You go on manufacturing machines that exhaust

your raw materials and huge amounts of capital; but you do not give the slightest assistance to the people who work the farms, where the world's real wealth is, and everything is going to rack and ruin.

You turn out graduates who will stay unemployed, bored and discouraged in your cities, yet you make no effort to train young people to love constructive, simple, craftsmanlike, agricultural work and to care more about a well-turned object or a loaf of wholemeal bread than they do about money.

If you need proof that you are on the wrong track, consider your unhappiness.

That will tell you the scope of your errors.

You are terribly unhappy.

Joy is a stranger to your homes, so well-built yet devoid of humanity and above all of humour.

But you have worked so hard. Do you not deserve at least a little peace in return for the effort expended?

And instead? ...

The trouble is, you measure everything by money, and this is a mistake.

Laissez-faire capitalism, having selected money as the driving force of its activity, is dying in disaster and shame.

Marxism seemed to have found a better way. In place of money, Marxism put labour. But it, too, has almost totally failed to understand the nature of man.

It, too, has violated human personality and created systems just as depressing and pernicious as those it sought to replace.

It is not much fun to tour a socialist city!

Just as it is not easy to breathe in certain areas of New York or Tokyo.

At least you ought to admit that you have been wrong, and that you still are wrong, that you are bunglers. And what is worse, that you prostitute yourselves all too readily for money.

Is this not so?

Your basic mistake is that you place money at the top of your scale of values, instead of truth and love.

After all, it is for money that you plunder the natural world, without the slightest thought that your errors will recoil on your own heads – as they are already doing.

But it is no good dwelling on the wicked past.

It would be better to spare a thought for the future, aware as we are that the conversion of human beings is not an easy matter.

Jeremiah said, 'The heart of man is incurable'.

In your position, though I am no economist, perhaps I would follow my ignorant intuition, not making five-year plans, but having only the welfare of mankind and the realities of the welfare of persons and of the world of nature in mind.

I would start by giving primacy to the countryside. I would consider cities the first mistake.

Why do the cities of Italy, of Brazil and so on, present the horrible spectacle of human beings jammed together in slums, living in subhuman conditions?

Because governments do nothing for rural areas, and the human beings who live there, afraid of being left helpless, flee in the hope of bettering their situation.

If governments gave minimal aid to the people who live in the country, and tried to give them a decent standard of living, most of them would stay to cultivate the land – which of course is ultimately what sustains all of you, even those of you who live in the city.

This latest, technological era of your history has seen an exodus from the countryside. The era of nonviolence, of which I dream, should see an exodus from the cities and a massive return to the country.

Country people ought to be helped to live even if all they do is to keep the trees alive or clean the irrigation ditches, thus protecting the land from destruction and neglect.

Make the land a garden, and the garden will become an Eden, giving you what you need: bread and peace.

If a youngster sells a motorbike to buy a bicycle, give him a reward. If a farm manages to get its electric power from a windmill or by burning waste, see that this is given public praise.

If enlightened industrialists start raising cattle or sowing their estates with spices, show your gratitude and knight them!

And another thing.

Litter-bugs should be arrested. And fine anyone cutting down a tree unless absolutely necessary.

A boy or girl who tramples a flower or torments a lizard should be sent to bed without any supper; and the politicians who have destroyed the olive trees on the plain of Gioia Taura should lose their salaries and jobs.

But you only smile. We are back in the world of *The Little Flowers*, I know. You do not believe in that!

I am a dreamer.

I am Francis of Assisi.

✳

But to leave ecology for a moment, and turn to men and women – it is they, and they alone, who are responsible for the problem of violence. In fact they are the only creatures in the universe that cause any problems at all.

Why are you so interested in the little story of the wolf of Gubbio?

Why have you fleshed it out with so many trivial details?

It interests you so very much – and yet it makes you smile. You do not really believe it.

In that little story you see the solution to the problems troubling you – yet at the same time you relegate it to the category of the utopias. A wolf tamed with a caress.

And yet, I have told you.

The miracle of that morning in Gubbio was not the conversion of the wolf, it was the conversion of the people who lived in Gubbio, who for a fleeting instant believed it was possible to overcome a wolf, armed only with food to give him instead of weapons to shed his blood.

Here you have the secret of everything.

Here is the absolutely basic secret, hidden in God's entire plan for humanity.

To believe in the possibility of the impossible.

To hope in things against all hope.

To love what does not seem lovable.

God's challenge to mankind is forever veiled in this mystery. And this is ever the substance of his request:

Can you believe?

Can you hope?

Can you love?

If you answer, 'Yes', I shall bestow the impossible on you.

Can you believe that God exists?

If your answer is 'Yes', then God certainly does exist – and you can sense his existence in your very faith.

Can you put your hope in eternal salvation?

Can you hope to be destined for a kingdom of truth, peace and love?

If you answer, 'Yes', then I shall make you smile with joy, and create a paradise for you where I shall be waiting for you.

Can you love men and women as I loved them, placing myself at their service to the point of dying for them?

If you answer, 'Yes', then I shall let you experience knowledge of God, since it is love that will lead you to him who is love.

*

The wolf of Gubbio is not a fairy tale for lulling children to sleep. It is the most extraordinary truth, the one that could save the human race, especially now when it is sitting on an immense stockpile of atom bombs.

All men see the image of the wolf in their neighbour.

If they allow themseleves to succumb to this fear and lose their heads, all is over. There will be nothing left to do but shoot.

Hence your danger is not in the wickedness of the Americans or the Russians.

Your danger is in their fear of one another.

I know the Russians and the Americans well enough to think that neither nation wants a holocaust.

But I know human nature well enough to know that if people are in the grip of fear they will try to press the button of destruction before the other can press it first.

Now that human ingenuity has reached the point of getting people what they want, and technology has removed their earlier limitations, the truth, the ineluctable truth, now becomes clear: that wickedness and violence are rooted in fear of others.

If human beings go to war, it is because they fear someone.

Remove the fear, and you re-establish trust, and will have peace.

Nonviolence means destroying fear.

This is why I, Francis, tell you this once again: Learn to conquer fear, as I did that morning when I went out to meet the wolf with a smile.

By conquering myself, I conquered the wolf.

By taming my evil instincts, I tamed those of the wolf. By making an effort to trust the wolf, I found that the wolf trusted me.

My courage had established peace.

※

You can deduce the rest by yourselves.

Just think what would happen if one day you became nonviolent, and took the huge sums of money you spend on defending yourselves against fear and used them to help the people of whom you are now afraid.

When your young people, dispirited by unemployment, and drugs, find their joy and vocation in helping the countries of the Third World, not only will you have solved the problems of others but you will also have solved your own.

You will know peace then.

Is it too much to hope?

Perhaps someone is listening to me!

To whoever it is, I, Francis say: Be brave!

ELEVEN

The Dark Night

The more years went by, the more I sought darkness and obscurity.

At first I attributed the phenomenon to a terrible pain in my eyes – due, the doctors told me, to diabetes. But eventually I grasped that there was something else invading my whole poor existence.

It was as if winter had got into my bones.

No longer did I thirst to see things. Even the sun no longer held its former fascination for me. Once it had betokened the Most High to me – thousands upon thousands of times. But now, when it touched my eyes, it spoke to me no more. It was as if the sun was now inside me, and had grown dark.

I nearly always prayed with my eyes closed now and I had an ever-growing sympathy with those brothers, especially the more mature ones, who preferred caves for their meditations and, even more, the darkness of night.

For years, daylight had afforded the most favourable conditions for my conversations with God, but now it was darkness that attracted me, and its murky mysteriousness.

The word had yielded to silence, and the silence now enfolding me had the rhythm of things repeated, measured by my breathing and my heart-beats.

'My God, my all,' I repeated, again and again. And that was really all I could say, for I was suffering intensely.

There was good cause for my suffering. My merry company was going wrong.

My spiritual family was divided.

The knights of my Lady Poverty were becoming more and more unfaithful to their bride.

I felt unable to do anything more for the brothers, that I had been wrong about everything and that time had ruined my dream.

Every day one friar or another would come to ask me whether it would not be better to change the rule, or to tell me that what was needed was common sense.

I wanted huts, and the houses around me became more and more like fortresses.

I had sought and loved companions like Juniper, Masseo, Leo, Giles – true sheep of God, simple as water – yet more and more cultured and cunning men kept entering our Order.

I could bear it no longer.

I went to seek comfort at San Damiano, where Clare lived in perfect poverty; and I was helped by her counsel to stand firm in the struggle. But my strength was waning, and I felt overcome by events.

The cause of my suffering was the opinion, shared by those who seemed most sensible in the Church, that it was impossible to live by the rule of perfect poverty.

It was as if they were telling me that the Gospel could not be lived *sine glossa* in its integrity on this earth, despite what I had always taught my brothers.

To me this sounded like treason against Jesus, in effect, doubting his word.

Once, when Christmas was approaching, I wanted to meditate on the life of Jesus as someone very, very poor. I set up a lifelike representation of the Cave of Bethlehem, at Greccia.

You see, I told everyone, you see it is possible. Jesus himself lived in this way. God became poor, weak, little, and gave himself into the hand of history, trusting only in his Father.

You see, you see, it is possible, since God himself lived like this!

But most people just savoured a bit of sentimentality, and everything threatened to end in rhetoric.

Faced with the facts, I heard myself saying: What is needed here is a little common sense. You see, Francis, the house will have to have another wing; let us have a little prudence, after all. And then, we need books, many books.

The brothers and sisters ought to be educated.

It is not enough to read the Gospel!

And perhaps all this was true. But I could not bear it.

I had understood and lived the word of Jesus in another fashion. I could not rid my ears of the refrain, 'Look at the birds of heaven ...'

This doubt in the ideal that had been my dream, this questioning of evangelical poverty, the sight of the friars becoming wise with the wisdom of this world, was unbearable to me and gnawed at my heart.

The pain of seeing my life's beautiful dream shattered was far worse than the pain caused by my diseased eyes.

*

Another source of pain for me was the mystery of a Church involved to an unbelievable degree in political strife.

To me, to be a Christian meant to be a witness to the tenderness of Jesus, a faithful follower of the lamb who went without bleating to the slaughter. And all around me, in the villages and cities where I went to proclaim the Word, all I saw were crosses on shields of steel, and swords, sharpened, as it was said, 'for the defence of the Church'.

Poor Church!

Poor Bride of Christ!

She herself, in full panoply, was preaching a crusade against the infidels, organizing alliances with the powerful, and involving herself in everything needed for victory.

Even the friars, my companions, whom I had so often told that our mission was to be meek and humble of heart, dreamed of crusades and would not have hesitated to take up arms against the Muslims, on the pretext of glorifying God by liberating the sepulchre of Christ.

Exactly where was it written in the Gospel that one had to liberate a tomb, even a tomb as illustrious as that of Jesus?

Politics was everywhere now, and everything gave way to that as though of right.

And my nonviolent ideal, my dream of going forth to meet mankind like lambs, was becoming progressively more tattered.

I even tried, in the midst of all this chaos, making a voyage to Egypt and to visit the Sultan Malik-al-Kamil – if only to show myself and others that there was no need to be afraid to meet the enemy unarmed.

But my mission did not succeed.

The Sultan treated me well, and I returned home without a scratch. But he was not interested in me. I would have preferred peace, but ...

I felt completely beaten.

＊

But where my bitterness overflowed all bounds was at the sight of the rifts developing in the Order and the intestinal strife now raging between the innovators and those who wished to remain strictly faithful to the rule.

The disputes over the rule paralyzed me. Unity was everything to me. Above all it was the sign of God's grace and loving response to our efforts to be faithful to him.

The sight of the divisions among us, the sound of Gospel texts being mouthed without meaning and twisted from their original simplicity, left me helpless.

I really felt as though darkness had fallen on what I held most dear in the world – my family.

At the Pentecost Chapter, held in May 1221, the very triumph of numbers increased my uneasiness. There were more than five thousand of us.

I no longer felt capable of guiding the Order. At the same time I wanted to keep a hand in everything.

Fortunately, I was thrust aside, and Fra Elias was nominated General.

Suddenly I felt better, relieved of a responsibility which had been weighing on me. But my peace did not last long.

The most intransigent, those who claimed to be the loyalest to me, returned to the assault, and the divisions became more acute than ever.

Francis, you must come back. You must take up the

reins again. You must make your weight felt.

Father, you must expel the most dangerous brothers ...

And on the other hand, those who thought themselves the pure, the spiritual ones, and who, making fidelity to the original rule their excuse, were becoming eccentric and unbalanced, lived in such a way as to attract rebuke from the Bishops by their inhuman penances and their wild and repulsive appearance.

No, I had certainly ruined everything.

*

Night had come.

The darkest night of my life.

Night without the presence of my God.

'My God, my God, why have you deserted me?' I repeated again, and again, like a dirge.

Still, the official approval of the Church, which Pope Honorius had been kind enough to grant me with the Bull *Solet Annuere*, brought me some comfort.

I went on visiting our various convents but could find no peace.

I would preach a little, then flee to some lonely hermitage, only to take the road again almost at once.

The place holding most attraction for me in those years was Mount della Verna, where the friars had built a small house and set up some peaceful little hermitages.

Mount della Verna was covered with woods. It had been given to us for prayer by Count Orlando.

I wanted to spend the feast of Saint Michael there, in one of those enormous clefts in the rock which had always impressed me, and which were said to have been produced at that moment in Christ's Passion when the Gospel says the rocks split apart.

The thought of the Passion pre-occupied me. I had a presentiment that I was about to fight the last great battle of my life, and that I should only find true freedom by identifiying my sorrows with those of Jesus.

With me were Fra Leo, Fra Masseo, and Fra Angelo. Fra Masseo acted as our guardian.

In their kindness, and knowing my tastes, my loyal friends had prepared for me the place that would suit me best.

They had gone ahead and thrown a little bridge over a crevasse in the rock, by which I could easily reach the chosen spot, which was an extremely lonely and quiet one.

It was Fra Leo who had the task of coming to me each day, bringing bread and water, and stopping at the bridge.

The password agreed on was the prayer 'Lord, open my lips' (Psalm 5:15). And if I replied with the other words of the psalm, he could cross and enter my cell; otherwise he was to turn back.

*

It was the dawn of 14 September, the Feast of the Exaltation of the Holy Cross.

The night had been a terrible one, and my prayer had been as bitter as death.

The temptation to leave the mountain, return to Assisi and resume the government of the Order had been eating at me with undiminished violence.

But now I understood that I was to live, within myself, the very sacrifice of Abraham. 'Sacrifice your son,' my conscience kept repeating, while the backlash of my wicked will urged me to action instead.

Sacrifice your son!

Sacrifice what you hold dearest - your Order, your life's dream.

What saved me in that moment was the thought of the Passion of Jesus.

How true it is that to solve our problems we have to get out of ourselves.

I forced myself out of myself and found myself on the way to Jesus' Calvary.

What was my sorrow compared with his?

What my defeat compared with his?

And who was I, vile little man, obdurate sinner, before the majesty of the Son of God, before the holiness of the Word Incarnate?

Before him, my poor scale of values was turned upside down, my story became trivial, my pains more trivial still.

And his presence became gigantic.

His word became more compelling.

He said to me, 'Francis, accept. As I accepted'.

I accept, Lord!

'Francis, sacrifice your life's work, as I sacrificed mine!

'Everyone betrayed me in the moment of trial.

'I was left alone. More alone than you, who still have friends on this mountain.'

Yes, I then felt the need to forget my own sorrows altogether and instead to offer myself to be permeated by and suffer those of Christ with him.

This prayer surged up explosively inside me, and this is how I still feel today:

Lord Jesus, two graces I ask of you before I die:
   First, to feel in my soul and in my body, as far
   as possible, that sorrow which you, sweet Jesus,

endured in the hour of your most bitter passion;
second, to feel in my heart, as far as possible, that
extraordinary love with which you, Son of God,
were inflamed, to the point of willingly enduring
so great a passion for us sinners.

Beyond the confines of myself, by his pure gift of
himself, I thus experienced the true mystery that rules
the invisible universe, had grasped, as only the poor
can grasp, the revelation of true love.

What counted in life was not to do, but to love.

What saved the world was not our wisdom or our
action but the power of the love of God, lived in each
one of us.

On the human level, Christ's life was a failure. But
on the level of his love, it was the masterpiece giving
new life to all creation.

By dying for love, Christ had raised the whole
world to life.

Death had been overcome.

*

I closed my eyes and let him do with me what he
would. The silence was complete. Even the birds kept
quiet although the dawn was sunny. Slowly, very
slowly, I felt myself being wrapped in a mysterious,
absolute embrace.

There came to my mind the words of Psalm 139:
'Lord, close behind and close in front you fence me
round, shielding me with your hand.'

After a while I was conscious of a very intense light
in front of me, and I opened my eyes.

I saw a fiery seraph. He had six wings. And he was
gazing at me more intently than anyone had ever done
before.

I had always thought seraphim would look like this, and I was happy that he was looking at me so intently.

And when I had thought of what contemplation must be, as a revelation of God, I had thought of it as something like this.

Meanwhile something was being branded into my flesh. And I did not know *where*,

or *how*,

or *why are you doing this?*

But I knew it was Jesus.

And he united me to his passion.

And he revealed the secrets of God to me.

No, a truer revelation than this could never be.

If the world had been created, this was why.

If Jesus had redeemed us, this was why.

If the Father always forgave us, this was why.

If the Church never failed on its march, this was why.

The embrace grew stronger than ever.

I felt a sharp pain, in my hands, in my feet, and even more acutely in my heart.

I felt the hot blood running down my body.

I could bear the pain no longer and yet was buoyed up by a presence that made me happy.

I understood then that I had found the centre of true happiness.

The solution to all anguish.

The open door of paradise.

*

Whether or not I had the stigmata was of no importance.

Whether or not I had open wounds, made by black nails, was of no account.

They would only have been signs, to be hidden as

much as possible. What mattered was that the fire of the Holy Spirit had penetrated my flesh, that same fire as had consecrated Christ on Calvary.

And it had made me his forever.

Now I understood why the world was so alien to me before I had experienced this adventure and felt this fire.

But I also understood that everyone, and everything, could be saved.

TWELVE

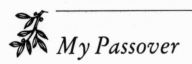 *My Passover*

Death could not be far away now, and henceforth it was easy for me to repeat:

> Such the joy that I await,
> that every pain is my delight.

The passage of the fire of the Spirit on my flesh had made the reality of things unseen infinitely clear to me.

Everything was normal again now. Nature was indeed the external sign of the things I had seen.

The course of the seasons, birth and dying, the rising of the sun and its setting: everything exactly betokened what the fire had shown me, the theme of the entire natural world.

Life and death were but two aspects of one and the same thing, as also sorrow and joy, light and darkness, cold and heat.

It was as though the real were cut in half by a door.

With good reason had Christ chosen the image: 'I am the door'.

The door is the same one on both sides.

The earth, the visible, the tangible, time and space,

are on this side; heaven, the invisible, the eternal, the infinite, are on the other side.

But everything is one, congruent, logical and true.

The door which is Christ simultaneously rules the here and the beyond with his love, crucified on this side, glorified on the other.

To become immortal and enter the glory of the Risen Christ, everyone must pass through this door, and the One who opens and closes it is the Lord. As Revelation says, 'If I open, no one closes'.

This passing is called Easter, and the first to pass was Christ the Lord – as it is said, 'This is the Passover of the Lord'.

Everything on this side of the door has its meaning, which can only be understood in function of, in the embrace of, what is beyond.

If unaware of this relationship, this continuity, you will never grasp what reality really is and will spend your life wandering in the dark.

Temporal things, if not referred to the eternal, make no sense. They are as nothing, dried-up leaves. Jesus himself said:

'Do not store up treasures for yourselves on earth, where moths and woodworms destroy them and thieves can break in and steal.'

And he added, 'But store up treasures for yourselves in heaven, where neither moths nor woodworms destroy and thieves cannot break in and steal' (Matthew 6: 19-20).

The resurrection of Christ gives meaning and life to every creature, created by the Father, and perfected by and through Jesus Christ.

And creatures, through him, have two aspects: one crucified, here, and one glorious, beyond.

Nobody can escape this fact, and hence the death of each individual has a sorrowful aspect in the here-now and a glorious aspect in hope.

Our passing is always a fearsome ordeal, like looking at a boundless sea – and then, the explosion of joy as you watch the sea part!

So it was for the People of God, and so it is for us.

There is always the painful wait, then a sudden light.

The wait is yours, the light is God's.

And it is free.

You can never claim you have deserved it.

On the contrary!

No merit has the power to open the door.

Only God's love freely given can manage this impassable lock.

'When he closes, nobody can open' (Revelation 3:7).

But his will is always prompt to open for 'This is why I came into the world, so that they can have life and have it to the full' (John 10:10).

How often have you asked, 'Why am I still here?'

And the reply is always the same.

You must learn to love. For beyond the door there is nothing – except love.

*

When I realized that I had holes in my hands and feet, and especially that I had a wound in my side, I understood what it meant to love without trifling.

Love is indeed a serious thing, a terrible challenge.

When I thought over my past life, from childhood to that moment, I could only feel myself to have been poor and sinful.

'Poor' now meant poor in love.

'Sinful' meant, 'You have trifled with someone who was suffering for you'.

The weight of this vision of things was terrible.

None the less these things are true, and we must not forget them too easily.

It is an ugly thing to step over the corpse of someone who has died for you, and to pass by singing when someone is suffering for you.

The law of love demands reparation. Instead, we forget all about it.

We should not be astonished if God sometimes makes us stand trembling at the gate.

*

After the Fast of Saint Michael in September 1224, I felt my passing was very near. Every least movement reminded me of it.

Since I could no longer walk, I rode a donkey. And ever before me I saw the back of Fra Leo, who had always been so devoted and so faithful, and who was the only person I allowed to see my wounds.

I hated it when people came to see me out of curiosity. I felt it was a secret meant only for me and Fra Leo, who had been with me at Sasso Spico and gathered me up in his arms like a wounded wretch.

Riding along, I joyfully saw my Umbria once more. The Marches too. And it was sweet to speak a word of comfort to those I met along the way.

Naturally I was a guest of Clare's at San Damiano and there I stayed a little while.

I felt so much at home in the little hut of branches which they had built for me against the wall. And at my ease being near so strong and good a woman, who had stayed punctiliously faithful to evangelical poverty.

When I looked at Clare all my problems disappeared. The brothers' everlasting arguments about whether or not it was possible to live poverty in real life, found their answer in the life of this creature.

Live, don't discuss, she seemed to be saying by her gentleness.

And there was another comfort for me at this period.

It was the answer to a prayer I had been making for some time now. I knew the answer would come.

God is so tender to us!

It concerned an ancient quarrel between the Bishop and the Mayor of Assisi.

How I had suffered because of it! For it was a scandal to so many. Besides, it seemed to me that Assisi ought always to be a city of peace.

Well, one morning I felt I needed to go into the city, and Fra Leo saddled up the donkey.

The wounds were hurting terribly, but I felt I had to go.

What a hubbub around me as I approached Assisi!

I felt the love of my friends closing over my pain.

What a grand thing, friendship!

How sweet, compassion!

Our route took us in front of the episcopal palace. I was motioned to go in; the donkey went through the gate into the courtyard.

I could not help but be surprised! Before me, side by side, stood the Bishop and the Mayor, looking at me.

I understood. They had made peace and wanted to tell me.

It was a beautiful thing. People were weeping for joy.

Then I opened my mouth and, in chorus with my brothers, with what was left of my voice, I sang:

> All praise be yours, my Lord,
>> for those who forgive for love of you
>> and endure infirmity and tribulation.
> Happy those who endure them in peace,
>> for by you, Most High, they will be crowned.

But now the time had come for me to pass through the door.

I had never been afraid of Christ, and after the revelation at San Damiano I felt him to be a friend close and true.

I even reached the point of being able to say, as true:

> Life to me, of course, is Christ,
> but then death would bring me something more.
>> (Philippians 1:21)

These words of Paul to the Philippians had always been a help to me. But now they gave me courage.

Meanwhile, however, I felt weaker and weaker.

I was surrounded with doctors. It became more like a siege, day by day.

Bishop Hugo wanted to lodge me in his own house, and for my sake made a pilgrimage to Mount Gargano, a place renowned in those days for its shrine of Saint Michael.

But I felt that the door was opening now.

I loved to recite Psalm 142, especially because of the mighty words that were now my continual prayer: 'Free me from this imprisonment' (Psalm 142:7).

Yes, this was how I would pray at my passing.

But for now I returned impetuously to my own

psalm, my life's psalm, which I myself had composed, steeping my pen in the beauties of my land, 'The Canticle of the Creatures'.

The canticle lacked its final verse, which I now composed and added to it:

> All praise be yours, my Lord, for Sister Death,
>> from whose embrace no mortal can escape.
> Woe to those who die in mortal sin!
> Happy those she finds doing your most holy will!
>> The second death can do no harm to them.
>
> Praise and bless my Lord, and give him thanks,
>> and serve him with great humility.

When I felt the hour had come, I asked to be carried to the Portiuncula, my mother church, the place of predilection, my Order's Bethlehem, my intuition of God's mercy and forgiveness.

On our way through Assisi I asked to pause a moment at the lepers' hospital.

My litter was placed on the ground and I asked to be turned toward the city.

I wanted to bless it. I wept and I suffered, but I was happy.

> God bless you, holy city,
> for through you many souls will be saved,
> and within you many servants of God will dwell,
> and from you many will be chosen for the realms
>> of life eternal.*

And when I lowered my arm again to my pallet a most sweet thought came over me.

I could not see the city towers, but I felt them as I breathed.

---

*This blessing is inscribed in Latin over the Porta Nuova.

I could not see Subasio, but I could sense its colour.
I thought.

The Most High Lord has made an exception for me,
Francis, but what an exception!

Scripture says, 'No prophet is respected in his own
country' (Mark 6:4).

And it says this to recall the mystery of rejection to
those who have suffered from it most.

Jesus himself knew the pain of being rejected by
Nazareth, his native country.

For me, Jesus had made an exception.

Assisi had not rejected me. On the contrary, it
loved me. And I too loved this little city, so lovely, so
gentle, so hospitable.

Then I was carried to the Portiuncula, where I
found myself the centre of affection, and where I
wanted to keep my own Passover.

It was a Saturday. A good sign! The third of
October.

I was almost entirely blind now; the life of my eyes
was already over.

Around me I could hear my companions. How
many there were! What rustling! What expectation!

It was like taking part in a solemn liturgical function, live as though in a cathedral.

As if I were the Master of Ceremonies, I asked to be
carried into the open air, under the trees.

They carried me out.

All around, the creatures, invisible to me now in
my blindness, spoke to me tenderly.

It seemed to me that they were praying with my
stricken friars.

When I realized that the hour had come, I ordered
them to lay me naked on the naked earth.

I say 'ordered', for it was not easy to make them obey.

There are always those who think of the 'passing' as something foreign, impossible, inappropriate, to be fled from. But no, here it was, and I desired it.

The moist earth gave me some relief. It was like a familiar embrace, beginning to enfold me once again.

But this meant nothing to me now.

The true embrace I now awaited from him, my Most High Lord.

I passed through the gate. It seemed to me I heard a choir.

Perhaps it was the angels of that little Church of Saint Mary of the Angels. It had always been my favourite one.

Praying with Saint Francis of Assisi

A Little Divine Office Composed from his Words and Prayers

I have tried to bring Francis of Assisi back to you. I hope I have brought him very near.

It has not been difficult for me to feel him alive, to hear his words as if they were being spoken now; for I am bound to him, and to the universality of his message, by love.

As I have already said, Francis is within each of us.

I was tempted to call this little volume *My Francis*, and this would surely have been more precise. I think, however, that each of you can do this: you can call it *My Francis*.

I have certainly not been very discreet in calling it *I, Francis*. Forgive me, if you will, for I hope I have been forgiven by Francis: in any case, now that my toil is at an end he invites me, man of high prayer that he was, to say some of his prayers with him (as a penance or as a reward, who can say?).

I admit I have drawn a few inferences. I have put his prayers together from here and there; but the prayers are his. And – inveterate monk that I am – I have arranged them in the form of monastic hours, a kind of Office composed by him, by Francis, that man of prayer.

To say that they are beautiful would be super-fluous. These are prayers written by a saint.

The Psalms, of course, are from the Psalter of the Church, but the arrangements of their verses is his and reflects his attitude of mind.

For each canonical hour I have selected a Psalm, a Reading taken from his works, and a Prayer.

The hours can be prayed all on one day, or they can be spread over several days. What is important is to be at peace and to read with a quiet mind.

INVITATORY HYMN
The Praises of the Most High

LETTER TO FRA LEO

You alone are holy, Lord God, Worker of Wonders.
You are strong.
You are great.
You are the Most High.
You are omnipotent, our holy Father,
    King of heaven and earth.
You, Lord God, one and three,
    are our every good.
You, Lord God, all good, our highest good –
    Lord God living and true.
You are charity and love.
You are wisdom.
You are humility.
You are patience.
You are safety.
You are peace.
You are joy and happiness.
You are justice and temperance.
You are the fullness of riches.
You are beauty.
You are gentleness.
You are our protector.
You are our keeper and defender.
You are our strength.

You are our refreshment.
You are our hope.
You are our faith.
You are our great sweetness.
You are our eternal life, great and admirable Lord,
   almighty God, merciful Saviour.

MATINS

PSALM

Shout for joy to honour God our strength, acclaim God with shouts of joy (Psalm 81:1; 47:1).

For Yahweh, the Most High, is to be dreaded, the Great King of the whole world (Psalm 47:2).

For the Father who is in heaven, our King from the first, has dispatched his beloved Son from on high, to be born of the blessed Virgin Mary (Psalm 4:12; cf John 3:16; Nicene Creed).

'He will invoke me: "You are my Father". And I shall make him my first-born, to rule over all kings on earth' (Psalm 89:26-27).

In the daytime may Yahweh command his love to come, and by night may his song be on my lips (Psalm 42:8). This is the day made memorable by Yahweh, what immense joy for us! (Psalm 118:24).

For the most holy infant whom we love has been given to us and born for us, on the road, and placed in a manger, since there was no room in the inn (Isaiah 9:6; Luke 2:7).

Glory to God in the highest heaven; and peace to men who enjoy his favour (Luke 2:14).

Let the heavens be glad, let earth rejoice, let the sea thunder and all that it holds, let the fields exult and all that is in them, let all the woodland trees cry out for joy (Psalm 96: 11-12).

Sing Yahweh a new song! Sing to Yahweh, all the earth! Sing to Yahweh, bless his name (Psalm 96:1). Yahweh is great, loud must be his praise, he is to be feared beyond all gods (Psalm 96:4).

Pay tribute to Yahweh, families of the peoples, tribute to Yahweh of glory and power, tribute to Yahweh of his name's due glory (Psalm 96: 7-8).

Offer him your lives, and bear his holy cross; fulfill to the limit his holy commands (Romans 12:1: Luke 14:27).

READING
The Praise of Virtue

I salute you, Regal Wisdom. May the Lord safeguard you with your sister, pure and holy Simplicity.

Holy Lady Poverty! May the Lord watch over you and your sister, holy Humility.

My pious Lady Charity! May the Lord watch over you and your sister, holy Obedience.

May the Lord protect all of you holy virtues, for you find your source in him and come forth from him.

No man in the world can possess you if he does not die to self.

He who possesses one of you, without offending the others, possesses all.

He who offends one of you lacks all and offends against all.

Each of you drives out vice and sin.

Holy wisdom confounds Satan and his wiles.

Holy and pure Simplicity confounds the wisdom of this world and the wisdom of the flesh.

Holy Poverty confounds cupidity, avarice and earthly cares.

Holy Humility confounds pride, all worldly men and all terrestrial things.

Holy Charity confounds all temptations of the flesh and the devil, and all human fears.

Holy Obedience confounds carnal and bodily desires and keeps the body in check. It holds us subject to the Spirit and obedient to our brothers. It keeps us submissive to all men in this world, and not only to men, but even to animals and wild beasts, to do with us what they please in so far as the Lord permits them.

PRAYER
(Letter of Saint Francis to the Chapter of Friars)

> Almighty, eternal,
> just and merciful God,
> grant to us wretches, by your will,
> to do what we know you wish,
> and ever to wish what pleases you:
> so that, purified in soul,
> enlightened within
> and inflamed by the fire of the Holy Spirit,
> we may follow the footsteps of your Son,
> our Lord Jesus Christ,
> and reach you, Most High,
> by your grace alone.
> For you live and reign and are glorified,
> in perfect Trinity
> and simple Unity,
> Almighty God,
> for ever and ever. Amen.

LAUDS

PSALM
The Canticle of Creatures

Most high, all-powerful, good Lord,
    All praise be yours, all glory, all honour
    And all blessing.

To you alone, Most High, do they belong.
    No mortal lips are worthy
    To pronounce your name.

All praise be yours, my Lord, with all your creatures,
    Especially Sir Brother Sun,
    Who brings the day; and light you give us through
      him.

How beautiful is he, how radiant in his splendour!
    Of you, Most High, he is the token.

All praise be yours, my Lord,
      for Sister Moon and the Stars;
    In the heavens you have made them, bright
    And precious and fair.

All praise be yours, my Lord,
    for Brother Wind and the Air,
  And fair and stormy, all the weather's moods,
  By which you cherish all that you have made.

All praise be yours, my Lord, for Sister Water,
  so useful, lowly, precious and pure.

All praise be yours, my Lord, for Brother Fire,
  Through whom you brighten the night.
  How beautiful is he, how gay, robust and strong!

All praise be yours, my Lord,
    for Sister Earth, our mother,
  Who feeds us, rules us and produces
  Various fruits with coloured flowers and herbs.

All praise be yours, my Lord, for those who forgive
  For love of you and endure
  Infirmity and tribulation.

Happy are those who endure them in peace,
  For by you, Most High, they will be crowned.

All praise be yours, my Lord, for Sister Physical
    Death,
  from whose embrace no mortal can escape.

Woe to those who die in mortal sin!
  Happy are those she finds doing your most holy
    will!
  The second death can do no harm to them.

Praise and bless my Lord, and give him thanks,
  And serve him with great humility.

READING
(Testament of Saint Francis)

Thus the Lord granted me, Fra Francis, to begin doing penance: when I was in my sins it seemed to me too bitter a thing to look at lepers; and the same Lord led me among them, and with them I experienced mercy.

And as I went among them, what had seemed to me bitter before, turned for me into sweetness of spirit and body.

PRAYER
Prayer Before a Crucifix

O high and glorious God,
enlighten my heart.
Give me unwavering faith,
sure hope,
perfect love,
deep humility,
wisdom, and knowledge,
that I may keep your commandments. Amen.

PRIME

PSALM

In you, Yahweh, I take shelter, never let me be disgraced. In your righteousness rescue me, deliver me, turn your ear to me and save me! (Psalm 71:1-2).

Be a sheltering rock for me, a walled fortress to save me! . . . For you alone are my hope, Lord Yahweh, I have trusted you since my youth (Psalm 71:3-5).

You have been my portion from my mother's womb, and the constant theme of my praise (Psalm 71:6).

My mouth is full of your praises, filled with your splendour all day long (Psalm 71:8).

In your loving kindness, answer me, Yahweh, in your great tenderness turn to me (Psalm 69:16).

Do not hide your face from your servant, quick, I am in trouble, answer me (Psalm 69:17).

Blessed be Yahweh, my rock . . . my citadel, my saviour (Psalm 144:1-2).

My Strength, I play for you, my citadel is God himself, the God who loves me (Psalm 59:17).

READING

And those who came to embrace this life gave everything they had to the poor and were content with a single tunic, bound if they wished in front and behind with a cord, and under-pants. And they did not wish to have more.

We clerics said the Office like the rest of the clergy. And we were very willing to stay in church, and were simple and subject to all. And I worked with my hands, and I wish to work: and I firmly wish all the other friars to work at an honest job, not motivated by love of money, but to set an example and to ward off idleness.

PRAYER

(Third Consideration on the Sacred Stigmata)

My Lord Jesus Christ,
I thank you
for that great love and charity
you show me.
I have learned that it is a sign of great love
when the Lord punishes his servant
for all his misdeeds in this world,
rather than punish him in the next.
And I am joyfully prepared
to undergo every trial
and every adversity which you, God,
are pleased to send me
for my sins.

TERCE

PSALM

Clap your hands, all you peoples, acclaim God with shouts of joy, for Yahweh, the Most High, is to be dreaded, the Great King of the whole world (Psalm 47:1-2).

God, my king from the first, author of saving acts throughout the earth (Psalm 74:12).

Let the heavens be glad, let earth rejoice, let the sea thunder and all that it holds, let the fields exult and all that is in them, let the woodland trees cry out for joy (Psalm 96:11-12).

Sing Yahweh a new song! Sing to Yahweh, all the earth! Sing to Yahweh, bless his name. Proclaim his salvation day after day, tell of his glory among the nations, tell his marvels to every people. Yahweh is great, loud must be his praise, he is to be feared beyond all gods (Psalm 96:1-4).

Pay tribute to Yahweh, families of the peoples, tribute to Yahweh of glory and power, tribute to Yahweh of his name's due glory (Psalm 96:7-8).

Offer him your bodies, and bear his holy cross: fulfill to the limit his holy commands (cf. Luke 14:27).

Tremble before him, all the earth! Say among the nations, 'Yahweh is king!' (Psalm 96:9-10).

And he ascended into heaven, and sits at the right hand of God, the Father most holy! (Ephesians 4:10; Nicene Creed).

Rise high above the heavens, God, let your glory be over the earth! (Psalm 57:11).

Cry out for joy at the presence of Yahweh, for he comes, he comes to judge the earth, to judge the world with justice and the nations with his truth (Psalm 96:12-13).

READING
(Testament of Saint Francis)

Then the Lord gave me, and still gives me, great faith in priests, who live according to the form of the Holy Roman Church, because of their sacred orders, and if I were to be persecuted, I should have recourse to them. And if I had wisdom to shame Solomon, and I found poor and humble secular priests, I would not wish to preach in the parishes where they were living without their leave.

And I will fear and love them and all their brothers, and honour them as my lords.

PRAYER
(Ubertino da Casale, *Arbor Vitae Crucifixae Jesu,* Book V, Chapter 4)

> May the burning and tender might
> of your love,

I beseech you, O Lord,
ravish my soul
from all earthly things:
so that I may die
for love of your love,
as you deigned to die
for love of my love.

SEXT

PSALM

May Yahweh answer you in time of trouble, may the name of the God of Jacob protect you! May he send you help from the sanctuary, give you support from Zion, remember all your oblations, and find your burnt offering acceptable; may he grant you your heart's desire, and crown all your plans with success (Psalm 20:1-4).

May we shout with joy for your victory . . . we boast about the name of Yahweh our God (Psalm 20:5 and 7).

May Yahweh grant all your petitions! Now I know that the Lord has sent us his Son, Jesus Christ, and that he will judge the world as it deserves (Psalm 20:5; cf. John 4:9).

May Yahweh be a stronghold for the oppressed, a stronghold when times are hard. Those who acknowledge your name can rely on you; you never desert those who seek you, Yahweh (Psalm 9:9-10).

Blessed be the Lord my God: you have always been my citadel, a shelter when I am in trouble (Psalm 59:16).

My citadel is God himself, the God who loves me (Psalm 59:17).

READING
To the Rulers of Peoples

To all magistrates and consuls, to all judges and governors all over the world and to everyone else who receives this letter, Brother Francis, your poor worthless servant in the Lord God, sends greetings and peace.

Remember and consider that the day of death is approaching. I therefore beg you, with all the respect I can command, not to forget the Lord, however embroiled you may be in the cares and anxieties of this world.

Obey his commandments, for all who forget the Lord and depart from his laws are accursed and will be forgotten by him. And when the day of death comes, all that they thought their own will be taken away from them. The more wisdom and power they enjoyed in this life, the greater the torments they will have to endure in hell.

And so, my lords, this is my advice. Put away every care and anxiety and receive the communion of the most holy Body and Blood of our Lord Jesus Christ in his holy memory.

See to it that God is held in honour by the people committed to your charge, and that every evening the signal be given by a herald or in some other way for praise and thanks to be given to the Lord God Almighty by all the people, And if you will not do this, be sure that you will be held to account on Judgement Day before Jesus Christ, your Lord and God.

Those who keep a copy of this letter and do what it says, can be sure that they have the Lord's blessing.

PRAYER

(Anonymus Perugianus, 10)

> Lord God,
> Father of glory,
> we pray:
> By your mercy,
> show us
> what we ought to do!

NONES

PSALM

Take pity on me, God, take pity on me; in you my soul takes shelter (Psalm 57:1).

Full of hope, I take shelter in the shadow of your wings, until the destroying storm is over (Psalm 57:1).

I call on God the Most High, on God who has done everything for me (Psalm 57:2) . . .

To send from heaven and save me, to check the people harrying me (Psalm 57:3).

May God send his faithfulness and love. He sends from on high and takes me, he draws me from deep waters, he delivers me from my powerful enemy, from a foe too strong for me. They laid a net where I was walking when I was bowed with care; they dug a pitfall for me, but fell into it themselves! (Psalm 57:3; 18:16-17; 57:6).

My heart is ready, God, my heart is ready; I mean to sing and play for you (Psalm 57:7).

Awake, my muse, awake, lyre and harp, I mean to wake the Dawn! (Psalm 57:8).

Lord, I mean to thank you among the peoples . . . your love is high as heaven, your faithfulness as the clouds (Psalm 57:9-10).

Rise above the heavens, God, let your glory be over the earth (Psalm 57:11).

READING
(From *The Little Flowers*)

Fra Francis and Fra Masseo arrived in a little village rather hungry, and, according to the Rule, they went begging their bread for love of God; and Saint Francis went by one road and Fra Masseo by another. But in as much as Saint Francis was a person of altogether humble mien and small stature, he was accounted a lowly pauper by those who did not know him, and received nothing but a few blows, along with some crusts of dry bread; but Fra Masseo, being a tall and handsome fellow, was given good bread, large pieces and even entire loaves.

Having gathered what they could, they met to eat at a certain spot outside the village where there was a beautiful spring with a large, beautiful stone, upon which each placed all the alms he had received. And Saint Francis, seeing that Fra Masseo's pieces of bread were more numerous, more beautiful and larger than his own, was highly delighted and said, 'Fra Masseo, we are not worthy of such a great treasure!' And he repeated these words several times, until Fra Masseo asked, 'Father, how can these be called treasure, when we are so poor that we lack the necessities of life? We have neither table-cloth, nor knife, nor fork, nor porringer, nor house, nor table, nor steward, nor maid!' Saint Francis replied, 'And this is what I regard as treasure: that there is nothing here provided by human industry, but that everything here is provided by Divine Providence, as is evident in the bread we have begged, in the stone that makes so firm a table, and in this spring so clear. And hence I wish the treasure of holy poverty, a thing so noble that God himself became its servant, should claim our whole-hearted love.' And these words said, with prayer having been made, and corporal refreshment having been taken of those pieces of bread and of that water, they got up and set out for France.

PRAYER

May the burning and tender might
of your love,
I beseech you, O Lord,
ravish my soul
from all earthly things:
so that I may die
for love of your love,
as you deigned to die
for love of my love.

VESPERS

PSALM

Sing Yahweh a new song, for he has performed marvels; his own right hand, his holy arm, gives him the power to save the one whom the Father has consecrated (Psalm 98:1; cf. John 10:36).

Yahweh has displayed his power, has revealed his righteousness to the nations (Psalm 98:2).

In the daytime may Yahweh command his love to come, and by night may his song be on my lips (Psalm 42:8).

This is the day made memorable by Yahweh, what immense joy for us! (Psalm 118:24).

Blessings on him who comes in the name of Yahweh! . . . Yahweh is God, he smiles on us (Psalm 118:26-27).

Let the heavens be glad, let earth rejoice, let the sea thunder and all that it holds, let the fields exult and all that is in them, let all the woodland trees cry out for joy (Psalm 96:11-12).

Pay tribute to Yahweh, families of the peoples, tribute to Yahweh of glory and power, tribute to Yahweh of his name's due glory (Psalm 96:7-8).

O kingdoms of earth, sing to God; sing to the Lord, who mounts above the heaven, of heavens in the east.

Listen, he will make his mighty voice heard; give glory to God for Israel: his power and his might are among the clouds.

READING
Concerning True and Perfect Joy

One day, in the vicinity of Saint Mary of the Angels, Blessed Francis called Fra Leo and said to him, 'Fra Leo, write'. The latter replied, 'Yes, I am ready'. 'Write', he said, 'what true joy is.

'A messenger comes, and says that all the masters of Paris have entered the Order. Write, "This is not true joy". Or again, all the prelates, archbishops and bishops have entered the Order – and the Kings of France and England to boot. Write, "This is not true joy". And if you should receive word besides that my friars have gone among the infidels and converted them all to the faith, or that I have received the grace from God to heal the sick and to work many miracles – well, I tell you, not even this is true joy.

'But what is true joy?

'Suppose that, returning from Perugia in the middle of the night, I arrive here. And the winter is muddy and so cold that icicles forming on the hem of my tunic are beating continually against my legs so that blood is flowing from the wounds they have made. And I, all in the mud and cold and ice, arrive at the door and, after knocking and calling for a long time, a friar comes and asks, "Who is it?" and I reply, "Fra Francis". And he says, "Go away, this is not a proper time to arrive. You can't come in." And when I persist, he replies, "Go away, you are a simpleton and a dolt. You cannot come in here any more. We do not need the likes of you." And I go on standing at the door and say, "For the love of God, take me in for one night!" And he replies, "I shall not. Go to the poor-house and ask there."

'Now, if I have had patience, and not become perturbed, I tell you, here is true joy, here true virtue and the soul's salvation.'

PRAYER

(Testament of Saint Francis)

> We adore you,
> Lord Jesus Christ,
> here, and in all your churches
> throughout the world,
> and we bless you,
> for by your holy cross
> your have redeemed the world.

COMPLINE

Who are you, Lord of infinite
goodness,
wisdom and power,
that you deign to visit me
who am a vile,
abominable worm?

PSALM

I give thanks to you, Yahweh, Father most holy, King
of heaven and earth, for you have comforted me
(Isaiah 12:1; cf: Matthew 11:25).

See now, he is the God of my salvation. I have trust
now and no fear (Isaiah 12:2).

Yahweh is my strength and my song, he has been
my saviour (Psalm 118:14).

Your right hand, Yahweh, shows majestic in
power, your right hand, Yahweh, shatters the enemy.
So great your splendour, you crush your foes
(Exodus 15:6-7).

The weak see this and rejoice. Turn to Yahweh and
your souls will live. Let heaven and earth acclaim him,
the oceans and all that move in them! For God will
save Zion, and rebuild the towns of Judah: they will
be lived in, owned, handed down to his servants'

descendants, and lived in by those who love his name (Psalm 69:35-36).

READING
(Testament of Saint Francis)

And the Lord gave me such faith in the Church, that I simply adored him and said: 'We adore you, Lord Jesus Christ, who are in all the churches of the whole world, and we bless you, for by means of your holy cross you have redeemed the world.'

PRAYER

(Third Consideration on the Sacred Stigmata)

> My Lord Jesus Christ,
> two graces I beg of you
> before I die:
> the first is that in my lifetime
> I may feel, in my soul and in my body,
> as far as possible,
> that sorrow which you, sweet Jesus,
> endured in the hour
> of your most bitter passion;
> the second is that I may feel in my heart,
> as far as possible,
> that abundance of love with which you,
> Son of God,
> were inflamed, so as willingly to endure
> so great a passion for us sinners.

WITH MARY

Greeting to the Blessed Virgin
(Opuscula, 123)

Hail, holy Lady
    Most holy Queen,
    Mary, Mother of God,
    Ever Virgin;

Chosen by the most holy Father in heaven,
    Consecrated by him,
    With his most holy, beloved Son
    And the Holy Spirit, the Comforter.

On you descended and in you remains
    All the fullness of grace
    And every good.

Hail, his Place.
Hail, his Tabernacle.
Hail, his House.
Hail, his Robe.
Hail, his Handmaid.
Hail, his Mother.

And hail, all holy Virtues,
    Who, by the grace
    And inspiration of the Holy Spirit,
    Are poured into the hearts of the faithful
    So that, faithless no longer,
    They may become faithful servants of God.